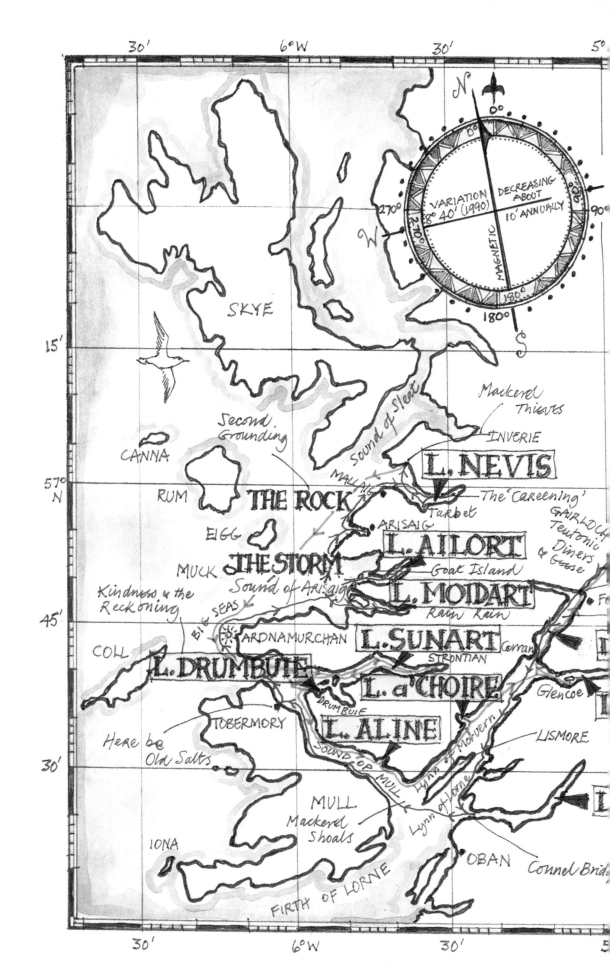

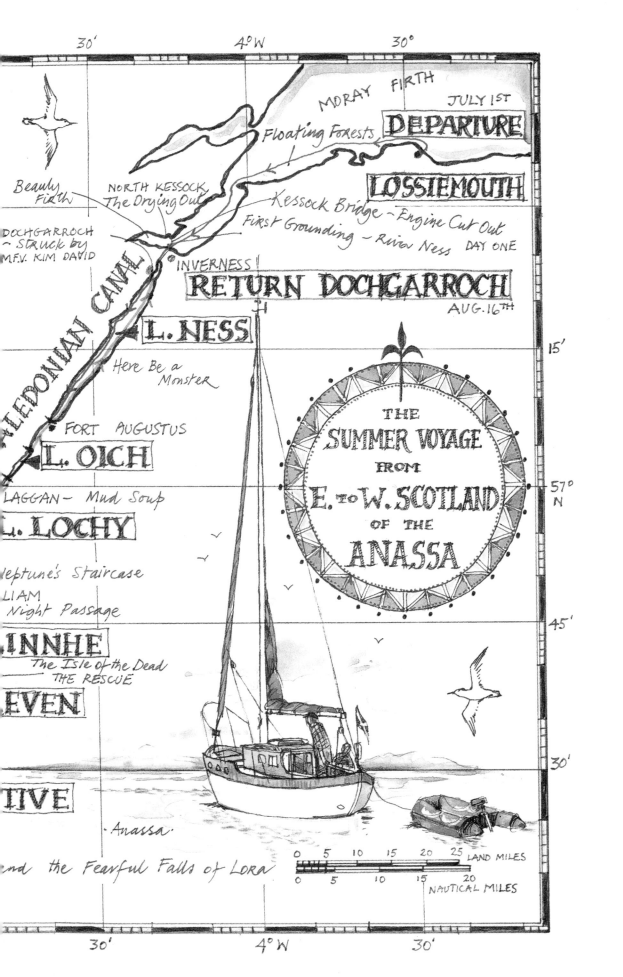

30' 4°W 30°

MORAY FIRTH JULY 1ST
DEPARTURE

Floating Forests

LOSSIEMOUTH

Beauly Firth

NORTH KESSOCK
The Drying Out

Kessock Bridge ~ Engine Cut Out
First Grounding ~ River Ness DAY ONE

DOCHGARROCH
~ STRUCK by
M.F.V. KIM DAVID

CALEDONIAN CANAL

®INVERNESS!

RETURN DOCHGARROCH
AUG. 16TH

L. NESS

Here Be a Monster

15'

FORT AUGUSTUS

L. OICH

LAGGAN ~ Mud Soup

L. LOCHY

THE
SUMMER VOYAGE
FROM
E. TO W. SCOTLAND
OF THE
ANASSA

57°
N

Neptune's Staircase
LIAM
Night Passage

INNHE
The Isle of the Dead
THE RESCUE

EVEN

45'

TIVE

· Anassa ·

and the Fearful Falls of Lora

30'

0 5 10 15 20 25 LAND MILES
0 5 10 15 20 NAUTICAL MILES

30' 4°W 30°

SEA CHANGE

SEA CHANGE

*The Summer Voyage from East
to West Scotland of the* Anassa

MAIRI HEDDERWICK

This edition published by
Birlinn Limited
West Newington House
10 Newington Road
Edinburgh
EH9 1QS

www.birlinn.co.uk

First published by Canongate Books Ltd, Edinburgh, 1999
Text and artwork copyright © Mairi Hedderwick 1999, 2009

ISBN: 978 1 78027 021 0

British Library Cataloguing-in-Publication Data
A catalogue record for this book is available from the British Library

Designed by James Hutcheson
Printed and bound by Bell & Bain Ltd, Glasgow

To the Captain

Contents

· Sound of Mull ·

'This narrow strait' (the Sailing Directions said),
'Is full of rocks and difficult to enter;
Whirlpools are common here at every tide;
There are unchartered reefs on every side
And currents (twenty knots) along the centre.'
'Come,' said the Skipper, 'we will go in there.'
(We went in there.)

'There is no sand' (the Sailing Directions said),
'The anchorage is thoroughly unsafe.
There is no shelter from the frequent squalls,
Save on the west, from overfalls.
Boats should go on to Loch MacInchmaquaif.'
'Come,' said the Skipper, 'we'll anchor here.'
(We anchored here.)

From *The Log of the Blue Dragon* by C.C. Lynam (1903)

Two kinds of women take to boats – those who like it
and those who fear to be left behind.

From *Better Small Boat Sailing* by John Fisher (1955)

Introduction

'*Anassa* can do anything; she can go *anywhere* ...' That is what the Captain said.

I had decided to leave the island, and live on the mainland. But before the transition, I had also decided, the water in between would have to be propitiated – slowly, lingeringly, and bravely. It would be a fitting farewell to the seascape I have loved and known so well for so long – but always with my feet firmly planted on the rock and sand of the island.

I am in awe of the sea; I am also frightened by it. 'But you lived on an *island*!' Ah, but that is the excitement of it! To be surrounded by such an element makes for a feeling of security – in storm or calm. To look out of a salt-encrusted window at a Force 10 in the bay, kettle bouncing and blistering on the hotplate, is quite the most secure of feelings. Equally, to hear the scritch-scratching of lazy sun-soaked wavelets on the shore, through wide-open windows in the long, light nights of June, that also confirms safe encirclement.

Travelling on CalMac ferries to and from the island held no fears. The ferries are deliberately disguised floating cafeterias and carparks and have no intimacy with the sea. And Samuel Taylor Coleridge did not write a poem about them.

Reading in rotation in class as a child it befell my lot to mouth these spine-chilling lines from *Rime of the Ancient Mariner*:

Water, water, everywhere,
And all the boards did shrink;
Water, water, everywhere,
Nor any drop to drink.

The very deep did rot: O Christ!
That ever this should be!
Yea, slimy things did crawl with legs
Upon the slimy sea.

The imagery had a lifelong and damaging effect on me. Always an imaginative child I pictured those 'slimy things' crawling up and over the gunwale of the boat – and me. Even now I will not swim in the sea if I cannot see the seabed; if a seaweed strand trailed over my leg I would surely die instantly of panic. And as for the things of the deep too unmentionable to describe, propelling their slithering slimy sinewy shapes to the surface …

There was a time when I valiantly overcame these fears. I inherited an 8-foot dinghy and half a dozen lobster creels. The chance to impress guests with Lobster Thermidor motivated much bravery. I never ever looked over the side, however, until the creel was just below the surface and was recognisably a creel and absolutely nothing else. As the lobster population diminished over the years, through commercial fishing I hasten to add, I became secretly relieved and enjoyed the dubious moral dignity of embargo.

But despite these fears, perhaps because of them, here I was, without any previous experience, preparing to undertake a six-week voyage on a very small yacht that would sail the waters in between island and mainland, and explore the fingers of fjords that indent the West Coast of Scotland. A seaborne foray of the mainland before the final parting. Like my Viking forebears I would stand proud at the prow of *Anassa* and survey new horizons. Be an adventurer in the last true wilderness – the sea, where there are no environmental pathways or perspexed maps, no cairns of stones to show the way or proprietorial signs of deflection, only the silver-pathed reflection of the moon of a night and the stars to guide the way. And there were charts like Ordnance Survey maps of the sea. The Vikings didn't have those. It would all be fine and very shipshape.

'She is a classical, seaworthy boat,' the Captain enthused. *Anassa* has particular and exotic origins. She is one of probably only six Lymington Slipway 5-ton cruisers built in the '40s and '50s: five built in Britain and made of English larch; the sixth, *Anassa*, built in Rangoon in 1954 and made of teak. *Anassa* is 26 feet long, with a 4-foot lead keel; roller reefing jib; mainsail; Lister 6½ hp diesel hand start engine; VHF radio; echo sounder; log; cooker; sea toilet; anchors and chain; Zodiac dinghy and 4 hp Seagull engine. A rare classic boat, right enough. The Captain knows his stuff.

The boat yard – The Slipway, Lymington – no longer exists; but the original plans for *Anassa*, designed by O'Brien Kennedy AMINA, are still in her chart locker. Why Rangoon? Two RAF Fleet Air Arm servicemen sent for the plans to Lymington whilst stationed in Malaya and had *Anassa* built locally; hence, teak instead of larch. There are handwritten specifications altering the keel and detailing white cedar wood and rosewood in the thwarts. But the predominant material is teak. Teak on teak; i.e. the ribs and planking are teak. This is unique. When I first saw her the hand-carved cleats and anchor rest caught my attention. They weren't just functional; they were sculptural. Everything about her is individual and personal.

At the end of their tour of duty, they sailed *Anassa* – no engine in her then – to Britain via the Bay of Bengal, Suez and the Mediterranean. She eventually ended up as a 'day sailer' on the cold North East Coast of Scotland. Four or five owners on, the Captain and I bought her. He'd been in love with her for years and wanted to give her freedom – the freedom of the West Coast. This ambition I shared in achieving in the weeks ahead.

Her name?

γουνουμου σε ανασσα. θεος νυ ιζ, η βροιος εσσι

Odysseus to Nausicca, princess (anassa) of Phaeacia:
Odyssey 6.149

***

First published in 1999, *Sea Change* charted a turn of a tide in my life. To have the opportunity, thanks to Birlinn, of going over the charts, so to speak, once again was a mixed blessing. But I think the yarn and *Anassa* have stood the ebb and flow of tide and time.

My thanks also to those who wrote with further information about *Anassa* on having read, often by chance, the '99 edition. The actual fulfilment of the RAF lads' adventure turns out to be a fantasy that came to us with *Anassa*. Relevant extracts from their letters are included in the form of a postscript. Who would have thought that a little boat could have such a particular and emotive history? Also included is a reprimand on behalf of King Canute (p54) and advice on the historical reference of the 'macintosh cloak' that most likely the knowing, not 'bemused', old *bodachs* in Tobermory knew all about (p87). And posthumous apologies are rightly recorded to the true poet of *Nimium Ne Crede Experto*.

Grateful thanks to the yachties who had the grace to say that all the mishaps we had are the ones they *all* have but *never* recount when back on dry land.

Very few of the illustrations in *Sea Change* are free sketches as they are in all my other books. I had to use a camera for reference. The reader needs to understand that often, like Daniell, I was in a moving, sometimes sloughing and bucking tiny boat. And was crew to The Captain.

And finally, thanks to *Anassa* who gave me a life-changing experience but who also gave those girls at Ballachulish their lives. *Anassa* was in the right anchorage at the right time.

A grand wee boat.

Mairi Hedderwick
Isle of Coll 2009

Departure: The Moray Firth

The car journey from Edinburgh to Lossiemouth would have been better undertaken by boat. Unprecedented high winds and torrential rain had made a waterway of the motorway. It was early July in the Highlands of Scotland. The undercarriage of the car soughed through puddles, and spray shredded off the windscreen wipers. Should I have already taken my seasick pills? It was late at night – too many well-wishing stops with friends along the way – and dark. There was a tide to catch at 4am next day; *Anassa* to victual and stow before then.

Flooding of the River Lossie caused country road diversions by Rothes and Elgin. The car was swamped on the stroke of midnight and refused to go any further. We were glad of our wet-weather gear. It was a precipitate christening for mine. A passing fire-engine crew en route to pump drains and remove fallen trees promised to phone the AA. The brilliance of flashing lights, shining yellow oilskins, red and silver glistening paintwork made me think of a lifeboat rescue. And we were still on dry land. It was a long wait.

'We'll not catch the tide. A day lost.' The Captain's voice stared into the whiplash night. Weeks of excited planning and farewells (some dramatic – the Captain did not believe in mobile phones aboard ship, or anywhere else for that matter) were ending in a puddle.

It was 2am by the time we parked the car at Lossiemouth Marina. *Anassa* bobbed gently, tied at her pontoon. Beyond the harbour wall the furies raged up the Moray Firth. There was time for second thoughts.

'And we were going to go out in that? In the dark?' I asked the bleary-eyed Captain.

'Just testing, just testing …' was his reply.

The day lost was in fact a blessing in disguise. I had only been aboard *Anassa* once before, many weeks previously, the summer's project a hazy dream ahead. Now I had a whole day to introduce myself to her.

I started by screwing in many large brass mug hooks – in a sort of affirmation of domesticity and organisation. The hooks were not for the mugs. They were in their little nonslip-matted cupboard – er, locker – behind the sink. All those bags of suntan lotion, Elastoplasts, vitamin pills, elasticated bandages, seasick pills, etc., etc., had to hang somewhere. The radio cassette merited two hooks, and so did the sponge-bags.

The herb garden – a collection of pots of chives, mint, basil, parsley and thyme – was watered, as were the sprouting seeds in their plastic pagoda. There was going to be no scurvy on this ship. By now the roar of the Firth beyond the harbour wall had become but a bluster, and the sun shone down on the herbs and the sprouting seeds on the doghouse roof. There was an air of *Swallows and Amazons* industry aboard *Anassa*.

Neither of us had discussed the expected role of the other. All I knew was that there was an awful lot of rope and sail activity going on up on deck and the Captain had indicated that nothing, but nothing, was ever to go on top of the chart table. I had indicated that nauticisms truly bored me but I would do what I was told when on deck.

I bent to cook my first meal on *Anassa*, bowed not with the inevitability of my lowly state in this naval enterprise but by the deck above my head. It took a while to remember to stand right into the doghouse when at the sink. It was the first of at least a hundred or so meals that I enjoyed creating; no tins or packets of soup, stew or custard in my galley. I love preparing and cooking food. It is pure therapy. Many times in the weeks ahead the retreat to the gimballed galley and the challenge of gourmet creations with two rings, a grill and billy-can container (remember, the Captain did not like mobile phones) superseded the seascape through the porthole.

Lossiemouth

There was cursing from above. The previous owner had removed the good-quality compass and replaced it with a waterlogged inferior one. But the Captain, being a hillwalker of repute, said he preferred his old pocket compass anyway. Reluctantly but sensibly, however, we had invested in a GPS (Global Positioning System). It was our one concession to modernity – unless the moist tissue wipes in the heads qualified. Both of us being computer fearties, we had not got the hang of it yet. Plenty time to conquer those inadequacies once we got going. It would be a long time before we were on the high wilderness seas of the West Coast. The straight-forward channel of the Moray Firth was tomorrow. A protracted progress down the Caledonian Canal to the West Coast at Corpach and Loch Linnhe. Even then there was still time to prepare before the real sea – the real sea between the island and the mainland that held the fears and monsters.

Anassa had never sailed on the West Coast. Neither had I. The Captain said that was what you called *real* sailing, none of this predictable East Coast stuff.

It is still night, but lightening, when the alarm goes off. 4am. Metal ping and tinkle of halyards all round. The whistle of the kettle on the stove. All else is silent. The storm is spent. Goodbye, *Knotsure, Lady in Red, Aphrodite, La Bamba* and *Itch.* You have kept *Anassa* company all winter and spring. She's off on an adventure all of her own.

Outside the high wall of the harbour we wallow into rollers, thick and brown-silted, from the swollen River Lossie. The swell is heavy across *Anassa*'s bow. A flat, grey opaque wall of sky meets the horizon to the East, shredding overhead into little cirrus dots over blue. Westwards the light is more enticing. We have got the tide right and are pushing up the Firth, making for the narrows at Fort George. We aim to get the slack in six hours' time to ease navigation under Kessock Bridge at Inverness, before heading for the entrance to the Caledonian Canal at Clachnaharry on the Beauly Firth. This, the Captain has worked out in great detail.

'You see, so much depends on the tide. Always use it. Never fight it. Go with the flow …'

The inshore swell left behind, the sea is now grey-green and calm. The old burgundy sails are listless. 'The early morning wind not out of its bed yet – still scratching,' the old salts say. 'It'll come by 10 o'clock if it is coming.' So often this adage proved true. The Lister engine thuds along at 4 knots. Conversation is impossible. Even the early-morning, low-flying jet practice at Lossiemouth is silenced. We pass Burghead and other ghost fishing ports on the south coast of the Firth. The white line of Culbin Sands, blanketed on top by the dark green of pines, slides by. By 10am we are passing Nairn. Time for a floating pit-stop and check on the diesel. Less than half a gallon used in three hours! Great little engine. Great little boat.

The sails still yearn for wind. We putter on through the grey-green silk water. Ahead there appears to be a flotilla of rowboats, folk fishing with rods high in the air. Slowly they drift nearer. They are giant trees half submerged, branches and roots akimbo. Eerily they pass. And more. They are further evidence of the storm floods. They are fully clothed in leaves, ripped untimely from banks of raging rivers.

'Hit one of those on a night passage at 4 knots and the boat would be in smithereens,' says the Captain. I vow that every passage from then on will be during daylight hours. *Anassa* has no radar equipment.

The narrow gap between the stiff-walled promontory of Fort George and the delicate finger of Chanonry Point is slurpy with little waves, indicating the slack of the tide already. The jib goes up. The Captain is determined to get up additional speed. We must get under Kessock Bridge narrows before the full force of the outgoing tide from the Beauly Firth 'attacks us'. His very words! The lack of wind from Lossie has slowed us down too much.

'But that little Lister will get us through, mark my words!'

I sit at the bow with my feet dangling down the open heads' hatch. The jib above is a rust-coloured canopy of colour in the grey liquid day. There is nothing for me to do, which is very pleasing. I think I am going to enjoy this voyage. The sun comes through the haze. Mercury flecks the littlest of waves. The Kessock Bridge is faintly discernible ahead. A couple of dolphins languidly arch through the water. *Anassa* pounds onward.

There is something ominous about the slack of the tide on a windless day. That is when its power is visibly recharging but with deceptive laziness. It takes slow deep breaths far below before slowly reversing its current of incontestable strength which nothing, but nothing, can halt or tame.

I thought of all the centuries of sea trade and invasion conducted entirely with sail power. I imagined little *Anassa* as my forebears' Viking longship, penetrating the upper reaches of the Firth on a day like today, just about to be inexorably and ignominiously pushed backwards by the turning tide despite lashing exhortation of the broken-backed oarsmen.

Or she could be the smack *Margaret* just last century, in 1884, praying for wind to fill her sails, for she would be laden with the first of the season's cargo of North Sea herring, hell-bent on reaching the markets of the Irish ports through the Caledonian Canal, which had opened two years previously. A good captain had to get the tide right, especially if there was no wind. He and his agent knew how much depended on it. With what foreboding those captains and their employers must have observed the first steam-powered ships slowly but steadily push against the outgoing force of water and gain harbour while they idled impotently, swinging at anchor, waiting for the tide to turn. Sail makers must have got wind of their own demise too.

We had an engine and we would make harbour in good time for the night.

By four in the afternoon we are close to the Kessock Bridge and lining up to go under. It has been a long, slow day of gentle acclimatisation and practical achievement. As long as I have not thought *too* much about pushing the tiller in the opposite direction to the direction intended, steering has been quite simple. The Captain says I can take *Anassa* under the bridge. Confidently I tussle against the rip tide which is already emptying the Beauly Firth into the Moray Firth. A tourist Dolphin Watch cruiser sweeps past down current at a prodigious rate. The passengers look seriously at our little bucking bronco, as does their captain.

High above, the commuter traffic builds up on the bridge. The activity is like a silent movie; we hear only the deafening racket of *Anassa's* engine echoing off the walls of the colossal pillars of the bridge.

Suddenly there is a split second of silence, followed by the collective 'om' roar of the traffic above and the turbulent slap and swirl of water below. The Lister has cut out. Just as suddenly I have no sense of control. The Captain flings off the engine cover as I am told to fling over the tiller and hold *Anassa* in line with what wind will fill the jib.

We have run out of diesel. Our cocky confidence in the old Lister's low energy consumption is to blame. The hard tack of fighting the tide latterly, albeit with the jib, had made for too greedy consumption.

The mid-channel pillars of the Kessock Bridge seem to close in. What a monumental height they are. The unsuspecting vehicles above seem to go faster and louder. The water churns on either side as we struggle under the bridge, yet also edge closer to one of the pillars. The daydream of lazy, hazy thoughts and progress has turned into a nightmare of uncontrollable sights, sounds and direction.

Refuelled, the engine will not start. The Captain hoists the mainsail for whatever drop of wind will keep us moving forward. We start moving backwards. I grip the tiller hard. Unbelievably, I have no fear. After all, I am not *in* the water, merely *on* it. At worst we will be swept back into the Firth and have to wait like the Vikings and the old fisherfolk until the next tide – as long as the pillars don't catch us. By now the tide race is licking round their buttressed pedestals. The Dolphin Watch cruiser cuts across the turbulence. It is obvious we are in trouble. I manage clumsily to get alongside. The Captain ropes on and we suffer the ignominy of being towed up the River Ness into Inverness harbour by a tourist craft named *Miss Serenity*, packed with camera-clicking holidaymakers.

'Well! We didn't see any dolphins, but we certainly saw you!' someone cheers. We have made their day, and off they go to their Bed & Breakfasts and fish suppers in jubilant mood.

Our mood is hardly jubilant. Here we are, tied to the high green-slimed walls of the industrial harbour of Inverness, where mounds of treated timber planks awaiting shipment block out the light and any view there could be. The only thing of note is the dramatic flow over the weir of the flood-swollen River Ness and the realisation that the tide of the Firth is now almost at its lowest. Less than half a mile away is the entrance to the Caledonian Canal and the delights of a tideless mooring, supper on deck as the sun sets behind the Beauly hills at the head of the Firth.

The engine still splutters non-cooperation, even after it has cooled down. The Captain repairs the broken facing on the gunwale where I came alongside *Miss Serenity* with too much enthusiasm.

'It is best these dramas happen at the beginning of a trip. Then they are over and done with.' He is rather nonchalant, I think. He patiently settles to clearing the air lock. He is finally rewarded. And relieved. For the harbour master says we must move; the sea cadet training sail ship *Royalist* is due at any time. Recharged with diesel and strong black coffee, we cast off and motor the short straight down-river before joining the Beauly Firth. There we will go to port, our backs to the previous blunder of the bridge, and make for the overnight mooring at the entrance to the Canal. It is long after closing time of the waterway. But we will be first in the locking through next morning. I tell all this in such locational detail, for it is essential that the reader can get the fullest possible picture and understanding of what happened next.

The Captain, with wise intelligence, gave me the tiller. I overcame my apprehension. It felt good. 'It's nearly low water. There will be little drag. I'll tell you when to put her about.' He pores over the Beauly Firth chart. There is a light early-evening breeze. The traffic on the bridge has slackened. There *is* going to be a sunset up the Firth. I am dying to swing her round and head westwards.

'Hard round to port!' the Captain orders. 'We're clear of the sand shoals at the river mouth.'

We are not. The previous night's storm floods are still determined to scupper our embryonic voyage of already epic proportions. With confident flourish I lean the tiller to starboard. Immediately *Anassa* is locked into a spin that has her ending up at a 70-degree angle to starboard. There is another split second of disorientation, followed by total incomprehension and panic. I scramble up the slope of the deck to the port gunwale, as evil swirling river water rushes over the starboard gunwale. Immediately the Captain is getting me into my survival suit and lifejacket. I'm incapable of any action save clinging to the rail and looking skywards. The inflatable

First Grounding
· Kessock ·

DAY ONE

dinghy takes for ever to unrope from the deck. The Captain's foot inflates it at crazy speed, at a crazy angle. I am waiting for *Anassa* to crack asunder or keel right over. Can I swim for the far shore, where people are already stopping their cars and staring? I will not swim over the yellow fingers of seaweed that dervish-dance along the submerged port side. How far will I have to jump to avoid them – and the rocks that will split *me* asunder?

There are no rocks. We are caught on the unprecedented stormflood-extended sand and shingle bar of the River Ness, where it meets the Firth, the massive weight of outflowing water clamping us securely, the prop half high and dry.

Once the dinghy is in the water and *Anassa* has not lurched or capsized due to weight redistribution (I still cling, high up, rigid to the stays), time settles as *Anassa* settles. Self-awareness starts to seep in. Quite an audience is collecting on both sides of the Firth. If the cars could stop on the bridge they would. I know many people in Inverness. They are all watching.

As the seconds of panic ease into minutes of possibly reassuring stability, only because I move not a muscle and shallow breathe, the Captain assesses our situation. 'We'll just have to wait for the tide to come back in and lift her off. No problem. Just patience.' That nonchalance again. Such sang-froid. How can he be so casual? Can he not see my whiter shade of pale, my pounds of instant weight loss? He is making coffee down in the 45-degree galley. 'Now this is when a gimbal really comes into its own!' He is laughing. Would you believe it?

As I relax my grip on the stays to take the extended mug, my knees trembling with loosening tension, I know it has all been my fault. Guilt floods in with the enervation. What damage has been done to *Anassa*'s keel and hull? My fault, my fault … I was at the helm. Silently we sip the warming brew. There is a chill in the air. I am not in the mood to see the humour of the situation. We will have to wait, exposed, in this crazy position, for at least three or four hours. I want to know if I will be needed when lift-off time comes; if not, I shall go ashore in the dinghy. Rat that I am. But on second thoughts that is more fearful to contemplate than enduring hours of creeping rising tide, for if I reach dry land, I know I shall not come back aboard – ever. Day one of the Voyage and I am quite ready to pack it all in.

'The humiliation! For all to see!' My tongue is loosening. On the South Kessock side, which is very near, young lads with mountain bikes have set up camp. Every so often they break from their virtual reality vigil to pirouette and prance on back wheels, whiling away the time before the obvious opportunity for salvage. The moving grandstand of motorised spectators persistently thrums over the bridge. I see someone waving. Is it my son? On the North Kessock side, the cottages with ringside seats for our first performance under the bridge have now, no doubt about it, set up free teas and coffees for the second performance. Binoculars included.

'Humiliation?' replies the Captain. 'Forget it. That is not the issue.' Cue for another self-enforced silence.

They say a watched kettle takes long to boil; waiting for the full tide takes six hours.

An inflatable from TS *Royalist* with a bo'sun and two cadets comes creaming over. The Tall Ship is anchored up-firth waiting for the tide too, but in a more elegant and composed manner. The cheery Bo'sun asks if we are all right. The local coastguard had alerted TS *Royalist*. I *knew* there were binoculars on us … That means we have been on every coastguard computer screen from here to Tiree, Ronaldsay, Dover and Scilly … Please, please, tide come in. This Viking no longer wants to stand proud at the prow of her ship.

It did, ever so slowly, oozing and slurping first onto the exposed mud banks behind. The lads had long since gone home to watch *Neighbours*. The Tall Ship glided by up-river to the harbour. Rows of bright orange lifejacketed young people hung over the side, smiling at our predicament.

Later the Bo'sun came back on his own, ostensibly to help pull us off when the time came but in effect, he admitted, to get out of galley supervision on the training ship. He tied on to the stern and chummed us for the remaining two hours. It was a welcome break from the silence that had descended upon the Captain and crew of *Anassa*. The Captain and Bo'sun had so much in common to talk about. Boats.

An almost imperceptible shiver along the length of *Anassa* indicated movement of the keel. There was an hour of stubborn immobility, still at 70 degrees, interspersed with fractious little jerks as she fought to free herself from the conflicting pressures of the down-flowing river and the incoming tide. Finally, with a wet scrunching sound she teetered, and comfortably but gracefully sank onto an even keel. It took several attempts to cautiously reverse her off the shinglebar, the Bo'sun over zealous to rev up the inflatable's high outboard. Strangely, those few critical moments were the worst. Was she going to fall apart at the seams?

- Drying Out . N. Kessock .

'It'll take more than that to break up that boat,' said the Bo'sun. 'Teak on teak, mm …' He'd had a great time, he said. 'Lucky devils. Six weeks on a boat like that on the West Coast … Lucky devils!' And off he powered in his state-of-the-art inflatable to the mundanities of Tall Ship management. He had certainly cheered up the Captain. All that nautical talk whilst waiting for the tide did wonders for the old sea-dog's morale.

It was 10pm by the time we tied up outside the sea lock at Clachnaharry. Both of us quite exhausted.

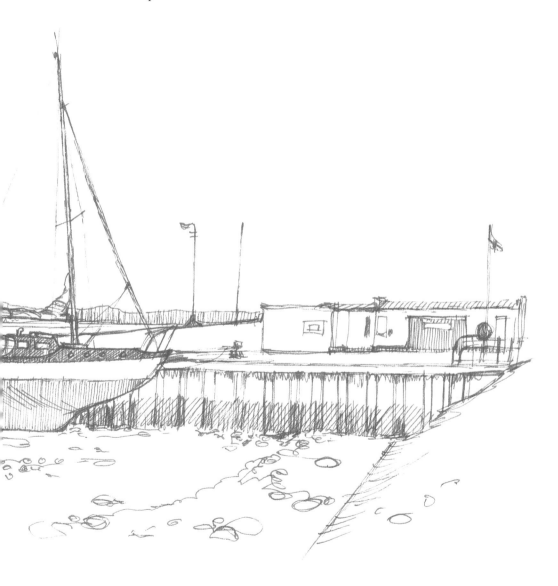

'It's not how I imagined it would be!'

'Ah! But you did see the dolphins, didn't you?' said the Captain. I had to admit that I had.

Thus ended the first day of the Voyage of the *Anassa*. Nothing else could possibly go as wrong.

Desperate as I was to get into the canal system and disappear as quickly as possible from the scene of the previous day's theatricality, the Captain with serious mien stated that he was not.

The lock-keeper had heard of our 'adventure' – who hadn't? – and was keen to talk. 'Happens all the time. We've told the Harbour Authority to put a marker at that exact spot. They're not interested in canal traffic. You'd better dry her out, just to make sure.'

This meant going across the Firth when the tide was high, tying *Anassa* alongside the old car ferry slipway and waiting for the tide to go down for inspection. Another day lost …

But it was a very reassuring exercise; there was no damage to the keel or even the paintwork. She looked very pretty, poised on the blade of her keel. Out of her element, shy to expose the elegant contours of her hull, determined to have dignity. We took advantage of her and scraped her underside free of all the winter barnacles. Many passers-by stopped to admire her. A local asked if she was for sale. I was still of a mind to consider such a proposal with alacrity, but the grey haze had gone and this slow day's healing sun was soaking up my lingering doubts. *Anassa* was obviously very special.

Once again at the end of the light of day and at full tide, we puttered over to the entrance to the Caledonian Canal, well pleased with ourselves and our caring for our much-praised boat. She was also our home. A bunch of wildflowers picked from the verges of North Kessock adorned the doghouse roof in a jam-jar.

The Firth was millpond smooth. The jewel lights of houses on both sides sparkled their reflections on the velvet dark water. The night was very peaceful.

The Caledonian Canal

The Caledonian Canal was opened to East–West Scotland maritime transport in 1822. Of its total length of sixty miles only a third is man made. A natural faultline of three lochs and linking rivers leading north-eastwards to Inverness, the Moray Firth and the North Sea and leading south-westwards to Fort William, the islands of the West Coast and the North Atlantic, was a God-given singularity just waiting to be developed into a commercial waterway in the days when travel and trade throughout Britain was conducted primarily by sea. Much sailing time could be shortened if there was naval access the length of the Great Glen. Baltic ships trading with the ports of West Coast Britain and Ireland and the British fishing fleet chasing the east–west migration of the herring would be able to save hundreds of miles by not having to go round the dangerous tidal waters and streams of the Pentland Firth and North West Scotland.

There was not only big money to be made from such an enterprise, but also military benefit. The ever-present fear of French invasion during the Napoleonic Wars would be greatly eased in the knowledge that gun frigates would be able to cut quickly cross-country, literally, at time of naval crisis whether on the west or east of the country.

The Brahan Seer had predicted in the sixteenth century that a time would come 'when full-rigged ships will be seen sailing eastward and westward by the back of Tomnahurich at Inverness'. Such an unbelievable sight was not witnessed for another century; even then, the first sighting of such a phenomenon wasn't seen here inland from Inverness. A certain Mr Knox, who had travelled extensively in the Highlands, wrote with passion in his *View of the Highlands*, published in 1784, about the benefits canals would bring to the area. He was responsible for founding and encouraging a Society for Fisheries and pushing for the building of the Crinan Canal in Argyll, which was finished in 1789. It was a much smaller and more local project, linking industrially developing Clydeside with the West Coast fishing grounds and obviating the long haul round the Mull of Kintyre. It was to be a further twenty-four years before the prediction and the dream of full-rigged ships passing eastwards and westwards through seas of barley at the back of Inverness would come true.

The man most famously connected with the building of the Caledonian Canal is Thomas Telford, although many others like John Knox and the British Fisheries Society had been campaigning and instigating surveys for years. Finally the Government committed itself to the project for all the reasons mentioned, but also to give much-needed employment, which would stem the depopulation of the Highlands devastated by the aftermath of the Jacobite Rebellions of 1715 and 1745. Forts George, Augustus and William still policed the wildernesses stretching east and west of the Great Glen, but the natives were quiet. They were destitute.

In 1803 the Canal was started from the Inverness end. Interestingly, the first proposed sea lock was to be the harbour; but the silt and shingle was too unstable. A blighted spot even in those days. The small fishing village of Clachnaharry was identified as more suitable.

Anassa was keenly first, stern flag fluttering, into the sea lock at Clachnaharry. The morning was bright and fresh. Her sensitised debarnacled hull gentled in the rush of soft fresh water coming through the lock gates, raising us up with giddy eddies of strength from sea level. It was the first of fourteen locks that would lift *Anassa* up the 106-foot 'hill' of the Canal to Loch Oich; fifteen more locks would then bring her down to the twenty-ninth, the sea lock at Corpach.

'This will be so good for her,' the Captain smiled. 'Nothing like peat water for preserving her timbers.'

I knew this bit of the Voyage would be good for me too. No tidal horrors. And no things of the deep. Just the odd trout or two that we would try to catch. I was conveniently forgetting about Loch Ness, which is 160 fathoms deep; deeper than the deepest part of the North Sea between Scotland and Denmark.

In theory the western seaboard can be achieved in fourteen hours; but, like a game of chess, there are so many moves and countermoves along the length of the Canal, some totally out of one's control – like lock-keepers' teatimes, cavalcades of campervans, cars and caravans at swing bridges and 50-ton cowboy-swaggering fishing trawlers – that it is best to take heed of the British Waterways Skipper's Guide which says '… but why rush? Relax and enjoy the delights of the Caledonian Canal.' We decided to do just that.

At Muirton we had to wait for a combined locking up through the four locks. The clam boat *Aurora* was first in the queue. She was from Orkney taking the shortcut to the West for clams and razorshells. The two lads had never fished, or rather dived, for that was their method, anywhere else but Orkney. The recent shellfish ban there on account of disease was forcing them into unknown waters. Their black dog, called Dog, was curled patiently in a box of ropes and floats.

It was historic to be alongside a working boat. With the dying of the very fishing industry for which it was part created, the Canal is nowadays predominantly used by yachts that transit the system and by tourist charter boats that cruise up and down its picturesque length. The Captain has great reservations about fishing boats in canals. But he said that the *Aurora* lads were not cowboys. You could tell by their island background, seemingly. Knew how to handle their boat in the tight confines of the Canal, you see.

Noella M, a posh vessel from Glasgow, and a Danish beauty of a big wooden gafferboat, which dwarfed *Anassa* not only by her grandeur but also by the blond rugged muscle of her crew and the long golden legs of their galley slaves, made up the locking foursome.

There is a definite style to locking. The style of all styles is not to motor through once the level is reached and the great gates open. Rather to walk the vessel with a guiding rope from the bow, a powering rope from the stern. Just as the canal workers, called trackers, did 175 years previously. They had to use horses for the big 100-ton barques, but *Anassa's* 5 tons glided effortlessly like a well-trained thoroughbred on a rein – two reins – as we walked her slowly from one lock to the next. Sometimes we were high above her, the ropes at full length, and the plan of her deck, far below, perfect in its elliptical confirmation; sometimes we were parallel with her. We, her trainers, proudly caught each other's eye but avoided those of the spectators in the enclosure, who had come to study the form before the race begins. Locking is a spectator sport too.

I soon learned all about posing during this slow, formal ritual of locking through. Why not? Everyone else did in his or her own particular way … Open water hazards past and, worse, those to come, just did not exist in this leisured space of self and boat indulgence. It is also a great opportunity to observe the 'yachtie' fraternity. The Captain had told me in the strictest terms that I was on no account to refer to ourselves as such. In all honesty I couldn't. Looking at *Anassa* corralled beside *Noella M* and the *Dutch Beauty*, glistening with all the panoply and accoutrements of high tech ownership, she had, despite her undoubted pedigree, more the air of a tinker's pony.

'All the more reason to have a pedigree!' expostulated the Captain, quite offended. 'Look at her! Pure Arab tinker blood.'

There was an exceptionality about her – and ourselves – that set us well apart from every yacht and yachtie we locked with or in the weeks ahead moored or anchored beside. The herb garden and the always renewed jam-jar of wildflowers; the ready-hooked fishing rods strapped on deck, their reels rusty with years of use; the homemade marker buoy for whenever I fell over the side, with large saltire flag disproportionate to the boat's 26-foot length; the fenders unmatching in colour and size; and open-fronted lockers round the cockpit displaying an assortment of diesel cans, bottles of paraffin, buckets of tools, spare anchor, lifejackets and harnesses, battery and basin of darrows and spinners – all connived to convey a somewhat worn and antique look. And that was all that was visible. The prize antique of all, the Seagull two-stroke outboard engine for the dinghy, was blessedly wrapped in a tarpaulin on deck.

The yachties' yachts always looked so immaculate. No gaping lockers. You could see through the prettily curtained saloon windows the plastic martini glasses neatly hanging from racks above plastic place mats depicting bright red crustaceans or navy-blue knotwork borders. Their ropes were all the same colour.

At Dochgarroch, a duck and her flotilla of ducklings joins ours waiting for the last gates to open before the channel of Loch Dochfour leads to Loch Ness. They bob up and down in the swirl of infilling water close to the centre of the great black gates that hold back the wall of water. They twist through the tiny crack at first opening, quaking with anticipation. The Dochgarroch moorings through the lock are a reliable source of bread. And showers.

It was ablution time and we parted company from *Aurora*, *Noella M* and *Dutch Beauty*, who creamed forward heading for the open space of Loch Ness. I suspect they had their own showers aboard.

Later, squeaky clean all over, three days accumulated washing festooned along the rails, ourselves and the ducks fed, a peaceful quiet extended as the Captain wrote up his Log. It was sundowner time. The *Jacobite Queen*, like a little Mississippi River boat, but which completely filled the lock, splashes by, towering above us. It is filled with evening cruisers going to see the sunset on Loch Ness. We raise our glasses to them as they raise theirs. 'Pretty boat!' someone shouts.

The next day being Sunday we decide to indulge in a late breakfast. The Captain even finds Sunday papers. 'Might be the last before civilisation comes to an end.' I can tell he is looking forward to such a lack.

There are many resident moorings at Dochgarroch and at weekends, what with the lock and the caravan site and all, there is much activity. Unashamedly lazy we lie in the cabin with yet another coffee, occasionally watching holidaymakers and yachts and cruisers go by through the wide-open doghouse doors.

'A bit like the Broads,' says the Captain dismissively, returning to the Travel section.

The morning is sunny and windy but a cloud comes over the porthole window directly behind and, irritated, I turn to see what has caused the change in weather. Inches from the circle of glass is a moving wall of rusty grey metal. 'God! It's a fishing boat,' I alert the Captain. 'It's *awfully* close!'

He is up and out in seconds: papers, coffee, croissants and jam in a mulch behind him. 'It's a bloody trawler!' he yells. *Kim David*, from South Shields, all 50 tons of her, has just come up from Loch Ness and is reversing from the shut lock gates where she has been blocking the Canal, engine running, waiting to be first into the lock when it opened. The lock-keeper is shouting at her to get back and tie up at the commercial jetty, which is next on from *Anassa*. 'Don't you know the rules?' The lock-keeper is furious.

The wind from across the Canal has caught the trawler broadside on and she is being pushed uncontrollably on to us. And I have got on only a big oversize T-shirt … I'm already in the water, knickerless, all my possessions floating on the Canal and *Anassa* in smithereens on the pontoon. The Captain does not feature in this disaster scenario, for in reality he is up on deck trying to hold off the massive weight of rusting hulk crushing down on us. Soon I am doing likewise. Futilely.

Shouting and swearing from the trawler sneers over our straining outstretched bodies thrust against her filthy hull, our hands red with rust flakes. *Kim David* is gaining the jetty but not without finally scrunching against us. More cause for hilarity from the trawler. Quite an audience has gathered by now on the bankside. Again.

The young, foul-mouthed crew of *Kim David* continue their abuse. The Captain has looked over the side and, thankfully, it is only *Anassa*'s paintwork that has been scraped. If she had been a plastic boat, it would have been a very different story. But the Captain demands to see their captain. The youngest and most obnoxious of the crew delights in shouting back, 'OK! Ya wanker! Come on then and I'll gi ya a fucking doin' o'er …' The Captain, till then only mindful of *Anassa*'s safety, leaps like a tiger from *Anassa* to the jetty to *Kim David* in two bounds. Obnoxious turns and flees into the wheelhouse and below decks like a rabbit down a hole. The rest of the crew hang heavy hands and look apprehensive.

Their captain surfaced at least. A civilised older man, who had no doubt been trying to ignore his crew's animal playtime, was willing to pay cash compensation for the extremely large quantity of International white gloss yacht varnish that the Captain estimated was needed to get *Anassa* back to her pristine condition.

The lock-keeper had more serious demands of him. *Kim David*'s insurance papers. These were 'not accessible'. All canal traffic must carry insurance papers. The lock-keeper had no authority to insist, but strangely he wasn't disconcerted by his apparent impotence. A jam of yachts and cruisers were waiting to get through on either side of the lock. What we didn't know then was that there was plenty of time for a phonecall to the senior lock-keeper at Clachnaharry, who did have authority. He would be waiting for *Kim David*.

The Sunday bunch of onlookers started to drift away. A local boat owner was delighted at the resolution of events. 'Happens all the time!' Where had I heard that before? 'The number of occasions I have reported that kind of behaviour. Fishing crews are not what they used to be. Some of them have never been on a boat before, let alone a canal.'

'There's another two coming up in a couple of hours,' said the lock-keeper. For him it was all in a day's work.

For the Captain it was time to cast off. 'We're not going to go through that again,' he intimated and headed *Anassa* down the channel towards Loch Ness.

I went below and put on my knickers.

The wind was bashing through the narrows at Dochfour. A Blakes cruiser came towards us at speed. 'Don't attempt Loch Ness. It is a cauldron!' the man at the wheel bawled. The summer-outfitted passengers were whey-faced, still shocked by the violence they'd experienced on the 24-mile journey from Fort Augustus at the other end of the loch. 'Mind you, it has only taken under three hours with that south-westerly behind us!' said the man at the wheel, relieved to be in the shelter of Loch Dochfour.

Anassa's practical speed of 4 knots would make little way in those conditions. We snuck into the eastside of the loch and found a magical little bay overhung with trees. The clear, still water was deep, close into the thickly wooded shore; beguiling paths wove in and around moss and pine-needled hummocks. This was more like the thing. A walk in the woods.

The Captain had other ideas. 'This is when we get to grips with that gizmo thing, the GPS.' I was dreading this. Our very life could depend on this technology and neither of us knew how to use it, being of, and stubbornly wanting to stay in, the era of star watching, sniffing the wind and steam telephones.

Global Positioning System is a computerised compass, navigator, plotter, tracker, speedometer, milometer and much more. Some can be the size of televisions. They are on CalMac ferries. Ours was the size of a big box of matches. Trying to programme it was almost as bad as setting the video recorder to record. And that is very difficult. I know. I thought I had got away from such tyrannies. It took us nigh on two hours to get the Little Bastard programmed. Tensions were high. I have a superior insight into these modern tools and remembered the never failing motto: It is never the computer that is at fault, it is the operator.

Dochgarroch

'*Don't* keep saying that!' The Captain was getting seriously angry as he tried to initialise the finicky piece of equipment. His great brigantine hands yearned to wind a windlass or scrimshaw a whale bone. I retreated to the bow with the jam-smudged remains of *Scotland on Sunday*.

In time the Captain said he thought he had got the hang of the thing. Now to practise the 'Getting Started Tour', as advised in the instructions. Where better than in the woods? I suggested. Dores Inn was on the other side.

Pulling the dinghy on top of moss and pine needles we set off, me reading out the instructions relative to the OS map and the Captain feeding in the data. We so seriously plodded, heads bent, through the unseen wood, up a track, onto the A862 and eventually to the welcome Inn. With the Little Bastard we were creating a sort of computer breadcrumbs trail that would lead us back 'home' to *Anassa*. Hansel and Gretel would have been so envious.

We assuaged an unconscionable thirst at the Inn. The Captain became increasingly confident of his newly acquired skill and looked forward to the return journey. I wondered what the wood had looked like. My neck was stiff and I did not like the idea of all those satellites up in the sky plotting my every move. What if I needed to go for a pee behind a bush on the way 'home'?

I was to read out the return route now plotted on the LCD, thus 'programming' the Captain who would lead the way. It was all so ridiculous. We knew the way 'home'. 'It's good practice,' the Captain insisted. By the time we got to the wood I was very bored. The Little Bastard was rigidly correct at every turn. I rebelled and lifted my head. That was when I noticed the plate-sized horse mushrooms at the side of the path. Then the chanterelles, orange fluted in the moss.

The Captain said he had really got the hang of the Little Bastard now and pocketed it. That was when he was free to find the blaeberries. Our first *au naturel* food-gathering! It was mixed mushroom omelette for supper; blaeberries and bruised oats soaked overnight in honey, water and rum for next day's breakfast. All this so nearly missed on account of the Little Bastard. The 'Getting Started Tour' ended with more rewards than one.

Loch Ness, Loch Oich, Loch Lochy

Early next morning the wind that had blown *Kim David* across the canal and the Blakes holiday craft up Loch Ness had not abated. The sun was gone. The deceptively sheltered channel up to Bona Lighthouse at the head of the loch did not prepare us for the full force of the south-westerlies in the open loch. It was going to be a long haul to Fort Augustus.

Spray broke over the bow as *Anassa* fought her way through large waves. I was not prepared for this either. This was, after all, an *inland* freshwater loch … Anoraks, leggings, gloves and headgear, a mug of hot Marmite and a thick cheese roll – it could have been January in the Cairngorms. Monticular cloud fingered the mountaintops on either side of the loch. They were like snowfields, the only brightness in a dull landscape. Banks of rain could be seen miles down the loch, making their drenching way towards us. The Little Bastard said we were doing 2½ mph, engine flat out. At this rate it would take us nine hours to reach Fort Augustus. *Anassa* lurched and bucked in the sudden squalls. The marker flag streamed out behind in line with the keel, straight as a die.

It was my first experience of trying to boil a kettle when all free-standing control of my body was impossible. A slight jack-knife posture wedged my girth between chart table, sink and cooker. With the engine thundering immediately to my right under the steep step out of the doghouse into the cockpit and the screaming whistle of the kettle I had found a Dante's Inferno of warmth and refuge. 'Honestly, it's no bother,' I would reassure the Captain many times that long day as I descended into domesticity. Snacks relieved the boredom of the passage. Chopping onions and carrots for soup was challenging; even more so the parsley. But much preferable to fixedly holding the tiller for mile upon mile with white-fingered hands.

The 24-mile long north-east to south-west trough of Loch Ness, with steep hills (Meall Fuarvounie is 2248 feet) on both sides, funnels wind from either of these two directions at a compounding rate. That and the estimated 263,000 cubic volume of water being pushed within a one and a half mile width can make for dramatic conditions. Water-spouts are not uncommon. We saw a few.

The maximum-recorded depth of the loch to date is 970 feet. The silt at the bottom is of unknown depth. Is that where the Monster lies torpid and sluggish in

between the sightings that have been recorded since the sixth century? St Columba described 'a certain water monster' in the River Ness in 565. In 1572 a 'monster' came ashore from Loch Ness, felling trees with its swishing tail, and killed three terrified onlookers. In 1871 Mr MacKenzie, thankfully walking high above Abriachan, looked down and saw a floating 'log of wood' or 'an upturned boat' come to life and move very speedily through the water. Such lengthy periods of hibernation this century do not seem to be the pattern. Recorded sightings in 1934, 1952, 1955, 1960 and amazingly every year from 1963 to '69 proved that the big sleeps were over. The monster had become more and more flirtatious, no doubt in response to the attentions of twentieth-century scientific investigation. Even allowing itself to be photographed and, worse, allowing images of its prehistoric dignity to be captured on key-rings and other tawdry tack. It had become a bit of

·Bona·
·Approaching Loch Ness·

a tart, really. An old tired tart; there have been no 'official' sightings of late.

'I once saw a monster, you know,' said the Captain as we slowly struggled past Castle Urquhart, where Nessie has been most frequently seen. 'A sea monster,' he continued. 'Touched it even. It was on the island of Ngazidja in the Comores. Loch fishermen had caught this large dark creature in their nets and were offering it for sale. It must have been about five feet long and weighed well over a hundred pounds. It had two pairs of fins beneath its body almost like legs. Its body didn't have scales like a fish, it was covered with large round blue discs. It looked as though it had been made out of pieces of enamel a long, long time ago. It clearly came from the sea. I imagined its crusty body moving slowly through the murky water of the deep depths as it had done for hundreds of millions of years, unchanged.

45 Fathoms

*'Entering the Reach
at Fort Augustus'.*

'I realised this sea monster was a coelacanth. Such creatures have been spoken of by fishermen in the Indian Ocean for hundreds of years, feared for their ancient strangeness and, in the past, quickly thrown back. I remember my youthful amazement at the whole idea of a prehistoric creature being discovered still to be living. Perhaps it is a legacy of this experience that I have never been in awe of science, rather fascinated by it, never believing it to be the sole property of scientists. It's a bit like poetry – belonging to those who read it, there for all to enjoy.

'The first coelacanth was caught in a trawler's net off the coast of South East Africa in 1938. Marjorie Courtney-Latimer, curator of the East London Museum, realised this was something unusual when she was presented with the remains. Professor J.L.B. Smith of Rhodes University recorded the very damaged specimen, naming it after Marjorie, *Latimeria*. He had to wait until 1952 before he was able to acquire another. Since then many have been caught; they have been photographed walking along the seabed.

'I didn't buy the wonderful creature. I was looking for a boat to get me home. A few hours earlier I had been aboard *Blue Lagoon*, a 36-foot craft, the property of a Seychellois pearl fisher. A huge, smooth-skinned, quiet-spoken man with a constant giocondo smile. I was the crew. Boat boy, actually.

'Well this vessel sprung a bow plank and began to go down. We reversed like fury towards the island. But she went down in minutes. No life raft, jackets, flares or dinghy for the pearl fisher. We swam ashore with nothing but his bag of pearls. And as we did so, curiously unhurried, he said, "Dammit man, that's the second boat that's gone down under me. Last time I had a much longer swim."

'He was a very fine pearl fisher but seemingly hopeless at choosing a sound vessel. Still I wouldn't have seen and touched a prehistoric monster otherwise.'

The Captain has done many and wonderful things. I hope this boat will stay afloat under him.

Our passage to Fort Augustus took seven hours and ten minutes. Long traversing tacks with the mainsail backing up the engine got us there just in time for the last locking up of the day with *Twilight Nectar*, *Glenfinnan*, *Santana* and *Seaspur*. Ironically the wind had dropped and an apologetic sun tried hard to shred the lifting cloud. *Santana* had sailed the East Coast of Britain from Southampton and the crew was bemoaning the fact that the weather had been against them all the way. Everyone agreed that it was the worst July for years.

Even more spectators line the edges of the five Fort Augustus locks. Our boats preen themselves for the 'walking through'. *Santana* is definitely the one and only pure bred Arab this time. *Twilight Nectar*, a wee sheltie rafted on to *Seaspur*, a bit of a Clydesdale. *Glenfinnan*, a Highland Garron, rough-coated. *Anassa*, the tinker's pony but with that Arab blood in her veins. 'Built in Rangoon, you say? My, my!' Well, it's near enough …

Large, modern classic yachts like *Santana* are like luxury cars. So much is press button activation. Even unto the saloon windows. Computers monitor and adjust and decide. Decks of digital display register all functions. There is central heating. On *Anassa* we sit at the helm open to the elements, 'in' the weather; hand crank the engine and light the oil lamps at night. But we revelled in our primitive princess holding her own not only with *Santana* but with the bevy of sophisticated beauties in the four other locks, totalling a mere quarter of a million pounds in value. We were in grand company. The spectators fancied *Anassa* again and again.

A wander round Fort Augustus Abbey brought the long haul of a day to an end. The slow mournful singing of Compline accompanied by an alto organ soothingly separated the secular wall-to-wall tartan of the village from the spiritual retreat of the Benedictine monks. Do they pray and mourn for the passing of their Abbey School, 1880 to 1993, too expensive to run latterly? Do they pray for, but ignore, the Heritage business that has not taken its place? Contemporary black marble slab Stations of the Cross with simple gold line carved images depict Christ's journey to Calvary. At the tenth Station, 'Jesus is stripped'. He has the cool attitude of a Levis' model waiting for his jeans to be returned from the stone wash.

The Log Fence · Kytra ·

We were well over halfway through the canal system and as though to cheer us on, the sun sparkled for us, the wind a mere zephyr. We let the pure Arabs, Clydesdales, Shelties and Garrons launch forward and enjoyed dawdling to single locking through at Kytra and Cullochy. They are one-manned locks with a cottage or two far from the traffic of the A82, its bus and car borne spectators ignorant of this hidden part of the Canal. It was as though moving from Fort Augustus we had moved backwards in time. It would not have been surprising if a tracker with his horse had offered to pull us through Loch Oich ahead or if the pretty little paddle steamer *Gondolier* had passed en route with Queen Victoria aboard. She would have waved a gloved hand. Like isolated but lovingly cared-for railway stations, Kytra and Cullochy are gems of individual and idiosyncratic landscaping. Recycled half tyres are painted brilliant white and jampacked with bright flowers. At Kytra, winter logs are part integral, part symmetrically decorational in the wooden fencing in the front of the lock-keeper's cottage. The logs look so old I have a notion log fires are a thing of the past and woe to anyone who removes but one from its artistic alignment. Nasturtiums trail everywhere over this sylvan Legoland.

Loch Oich. The summit level. From now on the locking will be downwards. It is the prettiest loch of the three that link the Caledonian Canal. Tree-crowned islands in the middle are meandered past within a narrow road of marker buoys, green to the south side, red to the north, where the tall tree-girt ruin of Invergarry Castle, burnt and deserted during the 1745 Rebellion, leans over the water to look at its own reflection, as in a fairytale illustration. It is as it was. In 1805 hundreds of workmen were drafted in to hand dig with pick and shovel the navigation channel. A dredging barge brought here at great expense had sunk. The loch was partially drained. The manpower proved ineffectual. It is the shallowest loch of the three and the one that cost Telford dear in time and money. It wasn't until 1816 that an experimental steam driven dredger was designed and built specifically for the task. The *Glengarry* could lift 800 tons in twenty-four hours. Imagine the noise and industry in and round the idyllic little loch in the hills at the time.

This brilliantly sunny day the loch was a hum of hire cruiser engines. To the south-west is the Great Glen Water Park, a triangular wooden chaleted watersports centre. There was talk of benefiting from its swimming pool but mud soup was waiting for us at Laggan.

Whether by land or water a stop-off at the *Scot II* café at Laggan Locks is not to be missed. Retired from her icebreaking role in the Canal this characterful little tug has ended her days serving all manner of sustenance to car and boat travellers alike. The mud soup? Delicious. The equally characterful owner has a reputation for homemade soups. 'Well, you know, you don't always get the earth out of the leeks, do you?' He was going ashore with a drained pot of chicken bones. 'For the hoodies,' he explained. 'Feed their wee chicks. If the lock-keeper's dog doesn't get them first …' Or the gamekeeper doesn't get Mr Mud Soup first.

The swans at Laggan are like the ducks at Dochgarroch. Startlingly white against the black-dripping wood of the shut lock gates, they know exactly the moment to glide through the opening gap. Another scruffy rude-crewed fishing boat coming north-east is idling, half barring our way as *Anassa* and *Sea Song* head

Mud Soup · Laggan ·

for the lock. The trawler is littered with beer cans. 'This generation just drink,' scowled *Mrs Sea Song*. She was quite capable of marching on to their boat and giving them a good talking-to in a motherly sort of a way. But she turned her attention to us instead as we twinned through the locks rafted on to *Sea Song*'s shimmering hull and stainless steel rail. 'Our first boat was an old converted ship's lifeboat.' She was being reassuring, implying that in time, we too – when we grew up – could be the proud owners of such a boat as theirs.

I look closely at her and work out I am as old if no older than she. I wonder at the years she has been a *Mrs Sea Song* and all the other mistresses she has been to her husband's other boats. Always crewing, never at the helm. Always trimly

First through
Laggan Locks.

trousered, neatly short-whitehaired. Adept at providing low cholesterol meals and washing the dishes with pink rubber gloves in a Force 8 gale. A methodical boat wife and meticulous chart reader. Always capable of washing the clothes in a pint pot. *Mrs Sea Song* has such a calm strength and undisputed experience. She moves about their boat with ease and quiet acknowledgement of her husband's instructions. She has so many skills I do not have. I long to ask the question that has started to wriggle into my consciousness. What will it be like 'out there' once the slow, safe (barring fishing boats) pace of the Canal comes to an end? But I do not have the courage.

Loch Lochy was all sun and glitter. Long like Loch Ness with sweeping mountains on either side. As we neared its end the biggest mountain of them all came into view. Ben Nevis. I tried sketching the shifting mass of it and the Nevis Range and remembered learning the reason why Daniell's engravings of the Western Isles and Coast of Scotland were so inaccurate: he sketched from moving boats.

It is seldom there is not a cloud shrouding the Ben. Its lumpen overall shape of elephant grey is arrested and creased upright on the North Face where ice-cold patches of snow still hold. Some years they survive the summer and become the base for the following winter's fall. And survive the next summer's thaw. And so on, and so on … The cable car pylons on Aonach Mor glinted with impatience awaiting this year's snowfall.

We had to accept a sardine pontoon berthing at Gairlochy with two other boats for the night, *Anassa* becoming a kind of cultural Berlin Wall. On one side was a hire cruiser with two young German couples. The men had the look and demeanour of pop group singers who stay in hotels like the Copthorne in Newcastle after a gig, swaggering, scruffy, really insecure in the milieu their success has brought. I think the girls did the steering when it came to the bit. On the other side was quite the most delightful couple, also German. Their tiny lacquered yacht, hand built by one of them in his garage – 'five layers crossed mahogany' – and trailered from Germany by the other, was set up for dinner alfresco with table and

Gair lochy
Greylags .

cloth in the equally tiny cockpit. The two elderly professional gentlemen come regularly to the Canal and spend the holiday going where the wind takes them. Every evening they wine and dine in formal style, each perched on the opposite gunwale of the minuscule craft, with silver service, a bottle of fine wine and classical music quietly playing. This particular evening the ceremony was bathed in the last of the day's golden light. A candle was lit. Like a lovers' gondola in Venice the very ripples of the water kissed time and them goodnight.

Very early next morning we crept on land to be free of the dominating bulk of the hire cruiser, appropriately called *Edinburgh Castle*, which had hung over our stern all night. The young still slept, windows steamed up. In front, the old sailors gently snored aboard their *Zephyros II*. An ice-cool satin mist curling in from Loch Lochy shivered and quivered on the surface of the water. Tame greylag geese silently wove in and around the dreaming boats, looking for breakfast. They followed us to a canal-side picnic bench and shared our bran oatcakes and honey. The silver satin mist evaporated at twenty feet where all was rust-gold, warming to the sun coming up over the Nevis Range. The mountains had a purple solidarity in silhouette. Trying to catch the perfect reflections of the Telford house and lock-keeper's cottage was impossible; wraiths of mist came and went, veiling the mirror of the lock basin. This was to be our last day in the Canal. By late afternoon we could be out to the sea loch of Loch Linnhe. I had mixed feelings. The leisureliness and sociability of the Canal would be over.

The Captain and I would be on our own.

8.10 am and we glide into the opening lock. *Edinburgh Castle* and *Zephyrus II* wave yawning 'goodbyes'. The mist trails us until the sun's heat kindles through. It is sunbathing weather on deck. Both of us take turns at the helm.

Whilst one drifts into water-lapped sleep, the other steers the straight road from Gairlochy to Banavie. Here the Canal is elevated over the valley of the River Lochy, which winds and snakes to the sea at Fort William. Man-made, the Canal heads resolutely straight in the same direction. To keep the level here, much of the

Canal is a landscaped aqueduct and only those who live around about know of the dripping green-slimed tunnels below, some wide enough to take a car, another with a 25-foot arch to let the River Loy thunder under in spate.

The morning had a celebratory feel to it. That summer's mid-morning feeling of well being, the rich reward of rising with the dawn; relaxation well merited and still a whole wondrous day ahead. If we had had flags I'd have dressed *Anassa* from bow to masthead to stern. We had coffee and cognac instead and returned to our private places only feet away from each other but in very different worlds.

We'd had a very hard start to the adventure but the last couple of days had stroked wounds and loosened tensions. I was not retreating to the galley so much. And from now on, weather permitting, evening meals would be up on deck not down in the dim, cramped cabin. I would buy a tablecloth at Fort William.

I was learning to accept the immutable position of the Master of the Ship and knew that it was important to accept this unconditionally before heading for the open sea. My observation of *Mrs Sea Song* indicated such. The Captain's sometimes-inexplicable vagaries were entirely due to my ignorance, I told myself.

· Banavie ·

I wondered what the Captain was musing on in this limbo passage along the Canal. He stood, the tiller between his legs, seriously, meticulously studying Loch Linnhe charts and tide tables spread on top of the doghouse roof, the box of herbs holding down the chart's flapping edge. This was definitely for the Captain's Mastery. I was going to go with the flow, tidal and otherwise, and turned my head to watch the gliding avenue of hazel, goat willow and beech trees, the hanging branches kissing and drowning at the touch of their liquid amber mirror image. I was the Ship's Artist, after all.

The engine revs drop down to tick over. We are giving way to two Tall Ships that come majestically towards us. Their broad girths almost the width of the Canal. *Jean de la Lune* is a nineteenth-century sail fishing bark converted for charter hire. Often she calls at the island on her way back from St Kilda and the Outer Isles. Has she been there this trip? Why do I still think of the island? *Agard Dublin*, much bigger, is a square-rigger, purpose built in Eire for charter. Not having been adapted and rejigged she is proportionally perfect. The wooden carved figurehead trails a Celtic pattern along the proud wearing of the green of her hull. As these leviathans pass I imagine similar ships passing with heavy dignity last century, towed by trackers and their horses; the crew relieved of duties up aloft, no longer clinging to lurching mast, crow's nest, stays or deck, battered by wind and wave. Limitless expanses of unpredictable ocean narrowed down to a stable pastoral passage, where the branches of canal-side trees brush the very rigging and wildflowers are almost within grasp. This idyll would take several days before the final towing into the Moray Firth, each ship let go with the tide and wind to her destiny.

Our contained idyll was coming to an end. Reluctantly I coiled the bow rope ready for the descent of Neptune's Staircase. I looked back, mile upon hazy mile, the length of the Great Glen and knew it was goodbye to the anachronism of boats inland.

The eight locks that make up Neptune's Staircase lower or raise boats 64 feet in 500 yards. Entering the topmost lock at Banavie to go down is exalting, like being on a diving board. At the bottom of the giant steps of locks is the railway and road bridge of Corpach, small below. The ocean pathway of Loch Linnhe beyond is like a runway waiting for our airborne landing. To the east the mass of Ben Nevis is diminished by our elevation, Fort William a toy town at its foot. *Anassa* is poised for the descent embayed in water, yet everything contrives to make her want to fly.

Neptune's Staircase is the dramatic memorial to Telford, his engineers and the thousands of labourers who built the Canal. Dropping down slowly lock by lock one can see the whole progress as if in a lift. Great square troughs of water, entirely

Top of Neptune's Staircase

controlled nowadays by hydraulic power, can lower and, most incredible, lift boats of several hundred tons the height of a seven-storey building. How much more amazing that lock gates were manned by hand with rotating capstans until modernisation in 1959–68.

Being one of the wonders of Lochaber, Neptune's Staircase is a magnet for tourists. Locking is in one direction at a time and takes about one and a half hours. If locking is in the opposite direction, double the time is needed. So this continuous water-lift in the height of summer attracts a moving mass of T-shirted mums, dads, grans, grandpas, toddlers and pushchairs. Foreigners with expensive cameras and long, cream raincoats jostle for shots, their sunspecs shoved to the dome of their heads. It is seriously crowded right to the edge of the locks, much more so than at Fort Augustus. No indulgence of posing here. Waiting for the lock water to drop is pleasurable and yachtie banter mingles with the outseeping. But walking through once the levels are equal is hazardous because of the eager jostling of the spectators, the downward sloping of the lock edge and my inevitable trailing rope.

The Caledonian Canal is due to undergo extensive repairs and modernisation and will be shut until the following May. I have a notion that Neptune's fork, with linking chain, will be replicated manyfold a couple of steps back from the newly masoned edges of his Staircase, leaving boat walkers safe room to pose again.

Loch Linnhe

Corpach. The sea lock. We are at the end. 'And at the beginning!' exults the Captain, who is definitely a sea-dog. But we do not sail off down Loch Linnhe to horizons new. 'Tide no use. It's too late for today.' I can't believe it. We moor at an ignominious pontoon beside the canal entrance and tell young lads to stop casting their fishing lines so close to *Anassa*. The white elephant cathedral of Corpach pulp and paper mill stands close by, a monument to latter-day investment in Lochaber. In about the same timespan as it took to build the Canal the mill was built, operated and closed down. Hundreds of workers were encouraged to leave southern Scotland and live in the area. The third displaced generation, if they are lucky, are employed in tourism. A residual force makes paper from imported timber. Were they responsible for the scummy surface that contoured round *Anassa* and the crabs that the young lads caught?

I was very discomfited and did not like this 'beginning'. But there was a tablecloth to buy and supplies for the galley lockers. 'This will be our last chance for several days,' the Captain warned. No more Mud Soup from the café bar of *Scot II* …

It was decided after victualling was accomplished that we would motor the ten minutes to Camus na Gaul, opposite Fort William, for the night. It was a perfect evening for sailing, the Captain said, but the tide would be against us at Corran Narrows. Well, why hadn't we got through the latter part of the Canal quicker, I peeved. It had been enjoyable going slow, remember, the Captain replied.

I sat with my back to the industrial and urban blots and traffic hum of Fort William, despite the dying arc of the day's sun behind the Ardgour hills spectacularly bronzing the hump and flanks of Ben Nevis like a Highland Ayers Rock, the close shadows of shore and woods of Camus na Gaul preferable. I couldn't believe it. Here we were, held in abeyance by a tidal activity nearly ten miles away down Loch Linnhe and having to endure a night of ice-cream van melodeons and traffic light cycles on and off, flashing through the porthole. The wind had dropped. A dropped beer can in Fort William could be heard across the water.

King Canute tried to control the tide. He should have tried to control the moon instead. All tidal forces are governed by the monthly cycle of the moon. Another reason why boats are feminine, I'm sure. The gravitational pull of the moon vertically attracts every drop of water in the ocean. Just as the moon waxes and wanes, so the height of the tide varies. Twice each month the full moon and new moon cause the highest and lowest tides, called springs. In between, the quarters of the moon cause the leanest difference. They are called neap tides.

Two high and two low tides each day on either side of the Atlantic are as sure as day follows night. But it isn't so in other parts of the world. King Canute would have needed to change radically the coastline of Britain and especially the West Coast of Scotland if, having accepted that tides are intractable, he had realised that he could get the least tidal variation by sticking Ireland back on to Scotland, Wales and England and putting the united landmass into the middle of the Gulf of Mexico, where tide rise is minimal. By rounding its outline to a complete circle with not one indentation he would have been able to reduce the rise even more.

The West Coast of Scotland is a littoral indented by hundreds upon hundreds of sea lochs and inlets. Islands of all sizes and shapes, some as deeply indented as parts of the mainland, shred off westwards. Sometimes narrow sounds and channels separate islands from mainland. Sometimes sounds and firths stretch broad in between. This irregular jigsaw-like fragmentation of land and sea is the cause of very varied and particular tide movements. The narrower the channel, the stronger the tide movement, as the massive weight of water behind rises to force through. The surface of the seabed also contributes. Deep flat it will allow the tide to flow or ebb unimpeded. A mountainous seabed with deep valleys causes turmoil and at high and low tide the underwater battle of wills manifests itself on the surface as well. Corrievreckan whirlpool between Jura and Scraba is the most famous example.

And as if all this isn't enough, there are the tidal streams, periodic *horizontal* movements of the sea; and with the wind and water inflow from the land it is enough to make one want to sail for ever in freshwater lochs. Or canals. The general direction of tidal flood streams on the West Coast is north, the ebb southwards. However, close inshore in some places, eddies run in the opposite direction. Where tidal streams meet, even if going in the same direction, overfalls, 'steps' of water, can occur. Charts of the West Coast are webs of tide and tidal streams like computer graphic images.

It is obvious to land souls like me what the wind can do to the tide. Push it or resist it. But in all the expanse of sea how can water from land affect the tide? It does. Heavy rainfall and snowmelt causing river flood can add considerably to the volume of the sea '… such as Loch Linnhe and Eil, it [the current] may be so strong that the duration and rate of the out-going tidal stream are naturally increased, and the in-going stream correspondingly reduced, or, in extreme cases, the stream may run continuously outwards.' (West Coast of Scotland Pilot)

Is mòid à mhuir Lòchaidh – The sea is the bigger of Lochy.

[*Gaelic*]

I had exhausted and terrified myself by all the reading. Old fears of the 'things of the deep' returned. Trying to understand it all made matters worse. One of the books said that we know more about outer space than we do of the seabed.

Fear is caused by ignorance. Somewhere deep inside me was a great but understandable ignorance compounded by a childhood insecurity that my mother would excuse to enquiring adults as I cooried behind her skirt saying, 'She is very sensitive.' It was the first big grownup word that had me flummoxed, but I *knew* what it meant. Later on I was described as 'very imaginative'.

Let me loose in the landscape and there are no emotional ghouls or bogies. Rather the opposite. The landscape frees me, welcomes me. I found that out in childhood, taking any opportunity to escape over the back garden wall from the claustrophobia of a middle class, single child upbringing. The Firth of Clyde was at the bottom of the hill but it didn't impinge on the sure comfort of the moors. What impinged more were the Christian overtones that underscored the week and dictated the lonely cleansing of Sabbaths. My African missionary grandparents and their transported artefacts at the back of every chair, behind every door.

In the Book of Genesis God creates the land out of a void and 'the darkness' that 'was upon the face of the deep'. 'And God called the dry land Earth; and the gathering together of the waters called He Seas: and God saw that it was good.' There is no sea in the Garden of Eden. Not even at the edge of it. But as we all know, things got rather wicked in the Garden. Without the anarchic and oft-times violent sea pounding on the undoubted shores of Paradise reminding man of his vulnerability? Hence the Flood. God's lesson to his first Plan A prototypes. The sea will engulf you. You have been bad.

When Noah and his family survive, God commands him to set about Plan B. A repeat performance of fruitfulness and multiplication of 'every living thing that is with thee, of all flesh, both of fowl, and cattle, and of every creeping thing upon earth.' But with the *exception* of the 'great whales, and every living creature that moveth, which the waters brought forth after their kind …' which Plan A, *pre* Flood, detailed. They, like the wicked of the world, were banished from whence they came and became monsters. On early maps the legend 'HERE BE DRAGONS' marked the unexplored edge of the sea.

Somewhere deep inside my antediluvian memory these monsters still exist. The coelacanth actually does. It was supposed to have died out 70 million years ago. Some 65 million years ago an asteroid strike is supposed to have killed off land monsters called dinosaurs. Another asteroid is predicted to collide with the Earth in 2028. The coelacanths survived the dinosaurs. Sea monsters clearly still remain. Undoubtedly they will survive this catastrophe too. It is obvious we should take to the water. But coelacanths are carnivorous, remember. 'Let's go, right now. To Corran.' It is almost a confrontation. I have to do something to break with this intensity of thoughts that will surely drag me down too far.

The Captain is exploring the sunset pinking of the Ben through binoculars, tracing old routes, plotting new ones. He looks at his watch. 'Nine thirty? It will take about three hours. You really want to?'

Is he daring me? Am I daring him?

What relief to be on the move! There is, of course, no wind. Except lightly at the bow, where I sit cross-legged looking down the length of Loch Linnhe to Corran in the late-evening distance. Hills to the east, like the Ben, pink gold. The Ardgour hills to starboard in shadow, their reflection on the loch black silk. Save for *Anassa's* slivers of wake there is absolutely no movement in the warm tail end of the sun-soaked day. The inflated dinghy is permanently on tow, no longer lumpen, a lifeless heap on deck. It lap-laps behind like an eager puppy. The sea passage has started.

'So has the night passage,' says the Captain, tying a red, spotted bandana round his neck. There is something ritualistic about this, I can tell.

A new moon comes up behind Treaslig, faint sickle etched into the apparently everlasting eggshell blue of the sky. A single seal bucks and snorts across our wake, smacks its tail in some sort of game with itself. From the land a sweet strong smell of honeysuckle – or is it bog myrtle? – floats over *Anassa*. The wildflowers in their jam-jar welcome contact with the land.

The pinprick light of Corran Lighthouse starts to show. We still have far to go. The moon is sharper white, the sky a denser blue. It is getting dark. I hadn't thought about that. I hid my uncertainties with nonchalance. After all, there had been a kind of mutiny. At least once. I had to follow through.

It was cosy in the cabin with the gimballed oil lamps as I read and reread the pilot book.

Corran Narrows. Tides – over 5 knots at springs. [O God, it was new moon.] Anchorages – *Corran Point*, north of the pier. Keep clear of car ferry moorings. Avoid both the shoal and very deep water on either side.

Corran Narrows.

Avoid underwater power cables. *Camus Aiseig*. There are many fish cages. Best anchorage is half a mile NW of pier, about half way between a stone slip and a group of houses at the mouth of a burn 3 cables further north. Don't go closer in than the 5 metre line as there are drying rocks on the low waterline.

By the time I got back up on deck the summer night had fallen. Black velvet hills, black velvet loch, a teasing turquoise sky holding light too high to be of any use for what I had committed us to. How would we be able to distinguish the detailed landmarks? We were close. It was possible to see the dark silent hulks of the moored car ferries ahead; the sweep of the lighthouse illuminated them rhythmically. I took the helm as the Captain tied the flickering hurricane lantern to the forestay. It certainly was not going to light our way. 'Night passage rule for identification,' explained the Captain. With the hurricane and oil lamp glow from the portholes the good people of Corran must have thought smugglers had arrived. It was the midnight hour. The channel buoy a mere twinkling little light half an hour ago loomed to port, a large ominous black structure that rose and fell, rose and fell. We thought we could see the long thin line of the shoal. With head torches we reread the pilot book. We could not make out exactly where we were. The Captain was reluctant to anchor without daylight and decided to chance a mooring near the shore. Professional yachtsmen *never* use unknown moorings. The owner could come back but, even more scary, it might not have been used in decades, its rope half shredded, its chain delinked with corrosion detaching from the weight on the seabed.

It was scary for me stretching over the bow, one hand holding on to the forestay just below the swaying hurricane lantern, the other gripping the boathook, waiting for the right second to hook in the mooring and slip *Anassa*'s bow rope through its ring. I'd had practice on the Canal, had got quite light of foot, almost balletic, leaping from the bow to the pontoon, whipping the rope round the cleat. But this was a very different kind of exercise. Of course, I missed the first time. Rigid with self-reprimand I waited while the Captain circled *Anassa*, her bow cutting into the fast moving black water. The tide had turned two hours previously and was building up a fine rate of knots as it forced its way to the Narrows.

It was a restless night. *Anassa* wallowed and tugged at the doubtful mooring. I could feel and hear the strength of the tide underneath her, underneath and alongside my bunk, wanting to envelop her and sweep her off to the Narrows. I dreamt frightening dreams that drifted in and out of wakeful spells when every yank of the bow rope was its last. Deformed babies floated by as I lay on my bunk, which was now in the wet oily womb of the bilges.

Terrifying dreams. Punishment for my earlier provocation.

But we managed it. A bit of a dual dare that paid off. And I had learned to read the charts and understand those tides and tidal streams. We never spoke of it again. Next morning the mooring turned out to be the fish farm marker buoy – one of the most secure you can get. The long thin line of the shoal, a row of fish cages.

It was a leisurely breakfast. We waited for the slack of the tide. There was time to study the charts and tide tables and plan the day's route and night's haven, hopefully more harmonious than the previous night's one.

The Sea Artist

Loch Linnhe is pinched at Corran Narrows then widens and slopes south-westwards to meet up with the Lynns of Lorne and Morven splintered by the island of Lismore. Eastwards Lochs Leven, Creran and Etive finger narrowly inland. Both of us had long harboured the ambition to drop anchor at the head of these and some of the other western seaboard lochs that run tendrils into the heart of Scotland's magnificent mountain areas. There is a particular perfection for me in the imagery of boats and mountains in juxtaposition. I was first attracted to the image seeing old engravings and aquaprints of the West Coast of Scotland. They were the first visual records that link in to my own after centuries of ponderous literary documentation, from Abbot Adaman, the chronicler of Columba, through Martin Martin to the arch tourist wordsmith of them all, Sir Walter Scott.

The Jacobite Rebellion of 1715 first prompted serious mapping of the Highlands of Scotland by General Wade on behalf of the British Government. The landing by sea on Eriskay in the Outer Hebrides of the New Pretender to the throne of Britain at the start of the second Rebellion thirty years later brought to the attention of the authorities their woeful lack of knowledge of the western seaboard. Martin Martin in his *A Description of the Western Isles of Scotland* (1703) had been telling everyone all about the inhabitants and geography of the area for years. He was a local from Skye:

Foreigners, sailing through the Western Isles, have been tempted, from the sight of so many wild Hills, that seem to be cover'd all over with Heath, and fac'd with high Rocks, to imagine the Inhabitants, as well as the Places of their Residence, are barbarous; and to this opinion, their Habit, as well as their language, have contributed. The like is suppos'd by many that live in the South of Scotland, who know no more of the Western Isles than the Natives of Italy …

Captain Durbé of *Le du Teillay*, a three-masted frigate with 67 crew, and the Bonnie Prince aboard, was a brave man. He had no charts like we had. He might have had aboard a copy of *Atlas Scotia*, first published in 1655, by Blaeu in Amsterdam, reissued in 1662. Timothy Pont, a Scot, was the source of this local information for the Dutch. The Dutch went before others to where there 'Be Dragons'. They were the masters of the unknown seas at that time. Was there a de Vries aboard *Le du Teillay*? Until a local pilot, if any, took over the helm it must, however, have been like a sea canoeist I once knew, who paddled the West Coast in the '70s with an AA map. As the canoe had no keel to speak of, the road map was more useful than any charts. Ports of hostelry were on road maps long before yachting became a recreational sport.

> Faosaidh luingeas 'mòr dol air taisdeal fada.
> Ach féumaidh sgothan beaga seòladh dlùth do'n chladach.
> Big ships may sail to distant strands,
> But little boats must hug the land.
>
> [*Gaelic proverb*]

Murdoch MacKenzie (b. 1712), an Orcadian, Hydrographer to the Admiralty and East India Company, produced the first charts of the West Coast of Scotland, after proving his maritime mettle by charting Orkney (the Pentland Firth was a Here Be Dragons cauldron) and Shetland waters. He started his survey of the West Coast in 1748 and finished nearly ten years later; nine months of the year aboard his survey ship, the remaining winter months in London, drawing up his detailed charts.

He worked on a grid of triangles 'pegged' by mountaintop cairns previously built by local labour. With sextant he worked out the angle. Imagine the days, even weeks, when visibility was nil.

It was no wonder it took ten years. On retiring in 1771, he still pursued his profession, publishing his *Nautical Description of the West Coast of Great Britain from Bristol Channel to Cape Wrath*. There is little information on his private life. I don't think he was married.

Later Joseph Huddart added to MacKenzie's life work. Huddart, who was from farmer-fisher stock in Cumberland, had gone into the fish trade, first owning and then building his own brig. The practical necessity of understanding and improving navigation during his working life became Huddart's new career when he retired in 1788. Philanthropist John Knox – of the British Fisheries Society, who was so keen on the construction of the Caledonian Canal (how the waters interweave) – employed Huddart to survey the Hebrides.

It was MacKenzie's charts that Thomas Pennant, Fellow of the Royal Society, used when he made his famous eight-week voyage to the Hebrides in 1772 on the *Lady Frederick Campbell*. He also employed the first recorded visual chronicler of this part of the unknown world. Moses Griffiths was a Welsh draughtsman and engraver from humble origins whom Pennant befriended and gave further training. Moses was a constant travelling companion, who must have known his place, however, on hearing Pennant describe his talented recorder as 'a worthy servant, whom I keep for that purpose'. The engravings are stiff and in some cases inaccurate. But I understand now the difficulties to be overcome whilst sketching from the deck of a moving boat. Also, those early artists could only reproduce by the engraving process. Some artists were not engravers and their original image was at the mercy of the hand and eye of the engraver who, obviously, had never been to the source location.

William Daniell was not an engraver foremost. He was a landscape painter. And it shows. After many years travelling in India with his painter uncle, also William Daniell, he established his name in the very popular Indian Landscape Painting market in England. Several paintings of Scotland, however, were exhibited at the Royal Academy between 1802 and 1807. Pennant's *Tour in Scotland* and *Voyage to the Hebrides* were received so favourably 'it [Scotland] has ever since been inondée with southern visitors.'

Daniell planned his *A Voyage Round Great Britain* in 1814. It was published in 1825 and, for me, his work is most attractive. The headland of *Ardnamurchan*, two brigs, perilously near to the swamping slough under a wall of delicately textured rock. A great shadow pales two-thirds of the face, pink-red mast pennants fleck life into an image that forebodes ill. But no dramatic colours or tones are needed. Delicacy, strangely, is the word again that conveys the message. *The Shiant Isles* is perfect stylisation, the disproportionate cliffs quite acceptable, their exaggeration not ridiculously gothic as later artists delighted in portraying, but elegantly monumental. Rafts and skeins of guillemots pattern the whole with humour. The ubiquitous boat tiny on its glassy sea. An even smaller one fades into the distance. Two plump geese or ducks perfectly parallel, in flight, the waterline.

Daniell was beneficiary of the new process of engraving called aquatint. As was John Clevely, a marine painter, son of a shipwright from Deptford, who captured sea images for Sir Joseph Banks in 1772 on his voyage to Iceland via the Hebrides and Faroes. Sir Joseph 'discovered' Fingal's Cave on Staffa, fair recompense for his disappointment in not accompanying Captain Cook again to New Zealand as he had done previously in the *Endeavour*. The exploration of the West Coast of Scotland was of equal importance to its discovery.

Another marine artist, Edinburgh-born John Schetky, who became Marine Painter in Ordinary (who was the Special one?) to Queen Victoria, braved the maritime elements with pencil and paper for the Duke of Rutland's *Cruise in Scotch Waters 1850*. As a lad he had been denied his dearest wish to enter the Navy by his musician father. Having inherited his mother's artistic abilities, he decided to paint the ships he would never sail in. Eventually he became Professor of Drawing at the Royal Naval College at Portsmouth. The cruise in 'Scotch Waters' must have been bliss.

Of these many draughtsmen, engravers, artists, Paul Sandby stands head and shoulders above them all. He was the pioneer of topographical art. Born in

Nottingham in 1725, he started his career like so many other artists as a military draughtsman, in his case in the military department of the Tower of London. After the '45 Rebellion he assisted in the military survey of the North and West Highlands. His maps and plans of castles and forts included locational elevations with identifying illustrations of land and sea.

He quit surveying in 1751 to concentrate on watercolour painting, which was in its infancy as an art. He became its 'father'. He did more than anybody at that time to draw people's attention to the beauty of the landscape and the capacity of watercolour to create the effects of light and air. This artistic understanding of the medium was unknown to draughtsmen of his day. Turner was a generation later.

Before Paul Sandby's time watercolour was only used to tint monochrome drawings. Colours were few and of poor quality. He experimented with pigments

Anassa. Lismore. '98 (56° 31'N 5° 29'W)

and also with a new way to reproduce originals. 'Aquatinta' he called it. A Frenchman Jean Baptist Le Prince had invented the basic process which Sandby perfected, after paying a fee. I'd like to think he saw and liked Daniell's rendering of the newly acquired art; but he died five or so years before Daniell's *Voyage*.

Aquatint is a form of engraving which differs from an etching, which is a straightforward reverse image in black ink on white paper to put it in its simplest terms. In an aquatint, spaces are left on the plate for the acid to bite into with less intensity to give the effects of washes or tints. In Sandby's time watercolour originals could not keep up with demand.

I know I am lucky to have the 100 percent reproduction of my originals nowadays, but there is a quality in those old engravings and aquatints that I envy. The reproduction is as much 'art' as the original.

I was fascinated by these first visual chroniclers of the seaway I was entering into. Disturbed to realise that those artists played the role of today's cameras and video recorders. But did they? The camera never lies. It just bores with its limited representation of landscape. I took my sketchbook out and tried to celebrate those visual chroniclers who recorded our first images of the West Coast of Scotland. Were they seasick? Were they frightened of Monsters? Were they servants like Moses Griffiths? Why were none of them women?

Like the Captain delighted in saying: 'Science appropriated their Skills and made Them, those Talented Men, its Own.'

Dear John Knox might have given us even more. He too was attracted not only to the economic but also the visual celebration of Scotland. He projected an elaborate work called *Picturesque Scenery of Scotland*, which was to be 'one of the most splendid publications ever attempted in this or any other country'. Joseph Farington, who had just completed a collection of engravings of English Lakes, and Charles Catton the Younger, who had travelled extensively in Scotland, were amongst those engaged to prepare drawings and plates. All this was abandoned when Knox died on 1 August 1790.

Despite being a slack tide the speed at which we flowed through the Narrows pre-empted any coherent sketch of the lighthouse and the mass of Gorbh Bheinn behind. The Ben shifted slowly but the lighthouse revolved like its prism.

Lynn of Lorne

Keen to get the sea wind in our hair and sails and tail we ignored the first opportunity to navigate inland to the hills. The entrance to Loch Leven was to port; the delicate tracery of the Ballachulish Bridge was fretworked, tiny below the tall obelisk of the Pap of Glencoe. We wanted to make use of the whole of the sun-glazed day, waves spitting diamond-splintered spray over *Anassa*'s neat little cleaving bow. Like a wee sea terrier she was off, unleashed, to the widening waterway of the Lynn of Lorne. Mackerel thralled to the gold glitter magnet of spinners on the line, twisting and turning with silver-flashing resistance. Supper was assured.

'We'll go into the hills of Glen Etive for the night instead,' said the Captain, exulting in the freedom. 'We should make the right state of the tide for going under Connel Bridge by late afternoon, then meander up to the head of Loch Etive and drop anchor below Beinn Trilleachan to the west, Stob Coir'an Albannaich a thousand feet higher to the east, Buachaille Etive More a little lower to the north. We'll practically be *in* Glencoe.

'There are ancient oakwoods, miraculously missed during the eighteenth-century pillage of timber for the charcoal factories of Bonawe. Ironically the charcoal leases that protected certain woods also protected them when landowners turned to the profits of sheep farming.

'I'll show you the rare butterflies that breed there and the seals that bask and sing to a backdrop of scree and heather,' went on the Captain. 'To walk into the head of Loch Etive from the mountain fastness of Glencoe it is so easy to think of the loch as freshwater. The sea *must* be a hundred miles away. I remember camping at the head of Loch Etive with a group of friends. We had been climbing in Glencoe and intended to ascend spectacular Ben Starav on the south side of the loch. Tents pitched, one of the team fetched a couple of dixies of water for a brew-up while others pumped up primus stoves. The water boiled while we chatted, easing toes from socks and boots. Tea leaves – no bags for real mountain men – were palmed into the boiling water. The infusion was allowed to mash before a little judicious tapping with a spoon on the side of the dixies drew the leaves in a centrifuge to the bottom. Tin mugs were filled, sugared and milked to taste and hand-cradled until drinking temperature was reached. All good thirsty hill men know the score; an anticipatory ritual like the hand rolling of a cigarette. The anticipation as delicious as the consumption.

That first tentative taste, tongue almost burning. It was *awful*. Undrinkable. The water carrier admitted he had not gone up-river to fill the dixies but had gone to the loch edge. A very high tide right up on to the grass, no seaweed or flotsam to warn, had persuaded him that it was fresh water. We called him the Seaside Mountaineer after that.'

The picture the Captain painted of this Brigadoon country was more fantastic than the Daniell images of sea and land I was already attracted to. It sounded wonderful. I knew a story about Deirdre of the Sorrows and her Nirvana in Glen Etive. I had to go there, for she is still there despite centuries gone. The loch and the glen the only witnesses to a mortal love and tragedy. I didn't know how the Captain felt about such Romantic notions, but he obviously was keen to get up Loch Etive. I'll tell him about Deirdre, I thought, when we feast off the Linnhe mackerel stuffed with parsley and thyme and gooseberry jam at the head of the loch. Always have gooseberry jam in the food locker on a boat for the mackerel.

The wilderness landscape of Morven opened up to starboard. Vast. Great tracts of land where no one appears to live, yet dotted along a single-track road system there are communities whose lifeline is totally dependent on that thin line. Gone are the days when all communication was by sea. And yet some places still need that sea link. As I write, there is the threat to close the Lochaline to Fishnish (Mull) ferry. This ferry is the only link for Morven schoolchildren to daily attend Mull's secondary school in Tobermory. Otherwise it means weekly boarding in Fort William to attend Lochaber High School. The weekend bus journey is eighty-odd miles return. Daily fresh milk deliveries from Tobermory to Morven will come to an end. Which is more important? Somehow, milk and schoolchildren go hand in hand. Neither should be penalised. Both are symbols of nurture and future.

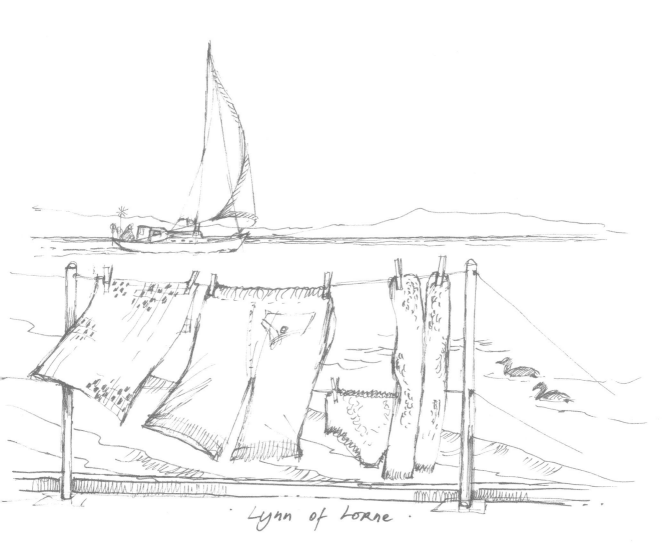

Lynn of Lorne.

Mackerel
for supper —
again.

Economics. The pink scar of Glensanda quarry where aggregate is quarried for the road systems of Europe and further afield. And the workers travelling by essential car have to loop into crumbling lay-bys to negotiate the oncoming Postbus.

It cannot be denied that Glensanda has contributed to the local economy. Some would say it has stabilised it. However, it is always questionable when one industry and only one is the main source of employment. Glensanda gives local work like the Canal did last century. But it is an extractive industry. The Canal in its origins, despite being political, benefited local people; the east–west fisherfolk, now the tourist caterers. Glensanda silently, loudly if you sail close enough, gives on-site employment only. I have to admit to the excitement of the drama of these wilderness hills, carved into a series of monumental platforms like a Cameron MacIntosh stage set for a Furies production featuring the Storm Witches Dodyag from Mull and Morag from Sutherland. It is the biggest hole in Europe, yet I find the scarring of its entrance visually exciting. There is talk of the same thing happening in Harris. Ochoin! Ochoin! Is it employment that is important or a landscape? The Caledonian Canal builders excavated and scarred the natural rift from Corpach to Inverness. Are they now forgiven because the ruptures are mellowed and mossed over?

Why do I feel that Glensanda and its dramatic reconformation of a mountainside is not a sin? Because it is out in the wilderness and is just a wee bit into the bigness of the land?

'And what will they do with it when they've extracted it all?' queries the Captain. 'Will they fill it with nuclear waste?'

Oh why is the Captain so serious? Wait till he hears about Deirdre, and the scar of Glensanda will fit into place quite comfortably.

I gutted the mackerel, putting them in a bucket of salt water in the shade of the doghouse. The second batch of sprouting seeds was ready for harvesting. Mackerel and salad for supper. But the dilemma: to pickle them in cider vinegar with onions or fry them in butter? The latter must always win for fresh-caught mackerel. The catch was so numerous there would be pickled ones for the next day. And the next, stir-fried for kedgeree.

One of the most satisfying experiences is to eat one's own garnered food. Both of us being 'foodies', the evening meal was the culinary climax to the day and much time was spent discussing the quantities, combinations and flavourings the galley locker stored. There was no fridge aboard so anything fresh had to be devoured to bloating point. There were sometimes several days between victualling forays to shore not only for food supplies but also for fresh water. *Anassa* had room under the cockpit sole for only two 5-gallon containers. Potatoes boiled in sea water are all right, but not much else.

The coolest part of *Anassa* was the bottom lockers under the bunks at bilge level, which I requisitioned for vegetables, dairy products, fruit and bottled liquids more flavoursome than water. Fine, as I discovered, until the day of the storm …

Days at sea in a small two-handed boat is an extreme test not only of the relationship of Captain and crew but also of their intestinal strengths and weaknesses. Can I hold it in until I get to land? There was a small pee bucket that had been originally filled with sweet eruptions of popcorn, its wraparound American flag label a reminder of desperate release on occasion. For more substantial needs there was *Anassa*'s teak-seated throne in the heads under the foredeck. Being small and used to crawling, the contortion of entering this private place was not too difficult for me. But the Captain is tall. Tall or small it was best to pull down trousers and knickers standing in the cabin before doing the twist. Once closed, a heavy tweed curtain hung on a half moon curved rail jutting into the cabin, hiding knees at right angles. On good days the hatch, inches above one's head, was open and with the littlest stretch even I was at eye level with the deck and the view.

Always a tense experience, I took to reading my book pretending my feet were not visible below the curtain. It became an enclosed space of privacy like the dry toilets at the bottom of the gardens not all that long ago, where nature and the elements were all around. A sea toilet has the added fearful element of the deeps down, down below. With particular emphasis the Captain explained the function of the flushing and discharge seawater pump action. If the seacock were inadvertently left open, the boat would go down, he warned. My tensions were not colonic, they were Titanic.

'Make the most of your time and comfort and privacy!' the Captain advised with a faraway look in his eyes. A story from a previous life was on its way, I could tell. 'I've used a thunderbox on a dhow. No privacy there. All it consisted of was four sides of a wooden box strapped to the tramsom. You divested garments and set yourself on this box over the stern of the vessel. No curtain! And you got wet if it was raining. The only concession to technology was a tin can on a string to bring up sea water to wash nether parts and hands. Mind you, no one on board would ever have looked at another on the box or have made any reference to it. So in an open and unrestricted way it had a kind of global privacy. It was wonderful at night once the strangeness of hanging out over the wake had been overcome.'

I was working on saving myself till the oakwoods of Loch Etive if at all possible.

Loch Etive

We were coming up to Connel, Ardmucknish Bay to port, Dunstaffnage hidden to starboard behind tall trees. I could feel another kind of tension gripping my gut. So many times we had gone over the chart and the pilot book, memorising the notoriously tricky and almost slackless passage under Connel Bridge, the entrance to Loch Etive. There it was in the distance tight like a virgin's hymen after the spread thighs of Ardmuchnish Bay and the folds of its bays within bays.

> If you are early, anchor off the Dunstaffnage Arms Hotel on the south shoreline [the pilot book instructed]. If you appear to be late, don't push your luck – the tide sets strongly towards the rocks on the south shore at the east end of the channel.
> Steer for the space between the bottom of the first and second oblique struts of the bridge from its south tower. There is no satisfactory mark for clearing the south end of the reef, but at low tide it is uncovered. Turn to steer diagonally across to the north shore; there is a submerged rock a little south of mid channel nearly half a mile east of the bridge. There are rocks off the end of Dunfiunary, a point on the south shore on which there is a house with a round tower, and violent eddies beyond it.

'We're early,' says the Captain and puts down the anchor. The water is oily calm, the sun is behind the haze. A Highland Heritage tour bus goes north past Dunstaffnage Arms Hotel. People wave from the windows. We are the only boat waiting to go into Loch Etive. I wish, so wish I was on the tour bus.

There was not a breath of wind and the slow swing and sway of *Anassa* at anchor had a doldrums feel to it as we waited for the tide to turn and help us navigate safely through these testing obstacles. Neither of us said a word during the vigil.

> Recommendations as to the time to pass the falls vary from half an
> hour either side of the turn of the tide to two hours, one figure being
> given by the owner of a sailing yacht with a small engine, the other by
> the skipper of a fishing boat.

'We've got a small engine …' I falter. And so it was with *Anassa* starting to severely buck and twist at the gathering power of the incoming tide meeting the continuing outflow of the loch, we pull up anchor and head for the hymen. Entering into the channel from the slow sidewater of the anchorage is like launching into a maelstorm. *Anassa* wallows and lurches and corkscrews and is very unhappy. I am rigid at the stern beside the Captain who obviously is having difficulty controlling the tiller, praying, praying, promising the Gods *anything* in return for this ordeal to be over. The horrors of the Kessock Bridge come back and hindsight has not dimmed total recall. I remember the fears of the men of Loch Awe, who were much afraid of the eels of Loch Etive which were 'as big as ane horse with ane certain incredible length'.

In almost slow motion, parallel to *Anassa*'s torturous twisting, a van parks at the side of the road; the workmen get out and settle comfortably on the rocks a mere 30 feet away from our performance. The audience had ringside seats. That's when the Captain turned *Anassa* round. Our gutless wee engine was no match for that force of water or spectator sport. 'They are locals. They know and we take their implicit advice.' The Captain said nothing more for a long time.

Anassa, relieved to be free of the challenge, headed happily back out to the wide waters of the Lynn of Lorne and Lismore. I was relieved too. Shaking with relief. Bugger the oakwoods of Loch Etive for butterflies or anything else. We were at Achnacroish on Lismore by early evening. The Captain still hadn't talked much. As we cruised for an anchorage someone shouted from the shore indicating a mooring. The Captain complied. He *must* be fed up, I thought. Little jellyfish floated by, their blue pinkness part of the pastel tonal day's ending that dusted over the hills of Benderloch and Etive. As ever in times of stasis it is best to lubricate the body. And we did.

The challenge of the two burner plus grill and the possibility of the gas running out at the most critical time, i.e. flambéing *les bananes*, is my kind of challenge. I can do a Greasy Joe of eggs, bacon, black pudding, tomato, potato scone, fried tatties, beans on such equipment and *everything* that should be is crisp and everything else is *not* tepid and everything is ready at the same time. The secret is a pagoda pile of dixies over one burner with varying stages of incubation. But much as we both needed a big fry-up that night the mackerel had to be addressed. They were quite delicious with apple and *Anassa* herb garden mint sauce oozing out of their bellies. Gooseberry jam drizzled to the side of the battered tin plates. All very nouvelle cuisine.

When Deirdre was born her beauty was there for all time. Not just in the perfect conformation of her body and face but in the glow and gurgle of her infant presence, presaging immortality. Whoever bore her knew they had a special child and political forces of the time used her arrival to disturb King Conchobar of Ulster in the guise of prophesy. It was prophesied that she would grow up to be the most beautiful woman in all Ireland and would destroy the House of Ulster. King Conchobar in the style of paranoid rulers the world over was too frightened to kill the prophetic child and took possession of her practically and hid her away until he could possess her literally. But when that time came and she was presented at court as his wife she fell in love with Naoise. The lovers fled Conchobar's wrath with Naoise's brothers and faithful warriors to Dalness in Glen Etive. A bit like Columba who had to flee political upheaval, Argyll was a safe haven. Peaceful. Somewhere to colonise?

Lovely its wood in the smile of the early morning,
A cattle fold of the sun is Glen Etive.

Of course Conchobar tracked them down and of course he promised Naoise and his brothers immunity if they brought Deirdre safely back to Ulster. Whether the rural idyll of Glen Etive was wearing thin or possibly Deirdre's charms, pangs of exile or local confrontation, the brothers agreed. Deirdre pleaded for them not to go back to Ireland. She had a dream of birds flying from Ireland to Scotland with honey in their beaks, returning with blood on their wings. Of course Conchobar had the brothers executed once he got Deirdre back. In time she died of grief.

From the hillside

Calls the cuckoo,
And methinks I hear it still.

Glen Etive,
Glen Etive,
Where I built my first bower.

Gaelic verse tells this story and it is the poetry of its telling that keeps the sad beauty of Deirdre of the Sorrows still weaving in and around the glen and loch of Etive.

'We'll go up Loch Etive on the way back,' said the Captain with a mouthful of mackerel.

The telephone box and postbox are conveniently together at the top of the Achnacroish jetty. The tide was no use for rounding Lismore into the Sound of Mull until later in the day. After a leisurely breakfast we rowed ashore with the ubiquitous postcards and made calls to the folk who wanted to know how we were getting on. 'Brilliantly!' we chorused.

We changed into walking boots and traversed the island well aware we had been boatbound too long. It was good to be in control of my mobility, no tidal race swirling round my feet. What delight in picking wildflowers for the jam-jar, collecting an armful of wild garlic leaves. We passed not a soul; it was not ferry time. We branched out cross-country. The Captain fell into a serious swamp; I managed to get electrocuted climbing over a fence. Like a couple of loony tourists we made our way back to *Anassa*. She had had a fine solitary break from us both.

The day was hazy again but with the bluer, cooler hint of a wind. The Captain looked forward to a bracing sail up the Sound of Mull. The south-west coast of Lismore

slipped by, the white weepings on the rocky shoreline evidence of the lime deposits that make Lismore one of the most fertile islands of the Hebrides. The wildflowers now jammed in the jar were certainly the largest of their species yet.

The Sound of Mull. A waterway of West Highland maritime history. What dugouts, coracles, longboats, galleons, through sail to steam puffers and now monster vehicular ferries have steered this channel? The monster ferries are as much part of its history of bloody battles and legends as those ships of the violent past.

Proof of this awaited us in Tobermory on the Isle of Mull where we were heading for the day's landfall.

Inevitably, the legend that most sticks in my mind is that of the lady of the Lady Rock, a rock covered at high tide half-way between the lighthouse tip of Lismore and Duart Castle on Mull. It is at the confluence of the waters of Loch Linnhe, the Firth of Lorne and the Sound of Mull. The conflicting currents when the tides are in full flood makes for turbulent boating even on the monster ferries. Here on this rock a MacLean of Duart tied his beyond-sell-by-date wife at low tide. He had found a fresher product. The rising tide, inch by inch, licked and slurped its ineluctable way up, up her struggling body. Thanks to the slow, yet inexorable, phenomenon of the tide, her kinsmen heard of the dastardly deed in time to row out and cut her free. The bitter waves were just brining her blue clenched lips.

Another self-imposed, self-indulgent build-up for a night of tidemares … Would I never learn?

As though to help me move forward in time yet still be part of my fantasy marine pageant, a black broad-hulled schooner with burgundy mainsail passed down the Sound. A hundred years ago the cargo might have been chests of tea, butts of claret, white procelain patterned toilet bowls for MacLean of Duart; today it carries four expensive Teflon-coated anoraks. Its mainsail was limp. As was ours. As we had expectantly plied into the Sound, the little tease of a wind had promptly died *immediately* we had put up the mainsail.

'That *proves* there is no God,' snarled the Captain.

Tobermory

Tobermory was on our itinerary primarily to see old sea-dog friends now retired from years of West Coast charter cruising. It was the last place we wanted to sail into especially on the eve of the Tobermory Regatta. But A and H would be a mine of information. A has forty years of experience of the vagaries of sailing on the West Coast catering for fortnightly boat guests. 'I seemed to spend all my time cooking,' rued H, who maintained she hardly got on deck. 'Stormy weather I hated, but there was a bonus. Nobody was very keen on food.' A belongs to a breed of sea farers long gone who navigated with limited technology and were pioneers of West Coast cruising. I have notes of my father's describing a sailing holiday starting in his home in Clyde that takes in the whole of the West Coast via the Crinan Canal turning back round Skye. He was but a 'cabin boy', but the journal has a tongue-in-cheek formality indicative of an easy familiarity with the element and situation he is in.

> So good had been our progress up the Sound [of Sleat] that we arrived at the entrance to Kile [sic] Rea earlier than we anticipated with the result that the ebb was still making; but it was the last of it and the Skipper of *Witch* decided to push on. Skipper never believed in an over-precautious policy because that did not yield the little element of adventure which he so dearly loved.
>
> [*circa 1919*]

MacIntosh Coats: Tobermory .

Save for the Little Bastard and the brand new Sowester marine battery linked to VHF and echo sounder, *Anassa* is similarly equipped to *Witch*. Sadly my father died when I was young, so I can only share the voyage of *Anassa* with him in the thoughts that end up on these pages.

A is Clyde-birthed and family too. In him I recognise the old traditions that we were brought up with of recording journeys with words and illustration. When he and H treat themselves to a winter cruise or travel to Canada or New Zealand to track down relatives and Mullachs (they are both very involved in the Mull Museum) A comes back with little notebooks of sketches in the Grand Tour manner. He shames me, for I have got lazy of late.

Though long retired from the wheelhouse, A still thinks and breathes boats and holds many a tale of West Coast sea lore. The Captain was eager to meet him. I was eager to get hold of H's bubble bath and running hot water.

Rounding Calve Island at 7 pm we saw the full flock of roosting Regattists. There must have been sixty or more boats in the bay of every shape and size and bank balance. Having been on our own solitary nautical idyll and the Captain, right from the start, totally against any radio contact with other boats or coastguard for chit-chat – 'Need to save the battery (unchargeable on *Anassa*) for emergencies only' – we were not prepared for the boat jam and had not got into Tobermory early enough to get an anchorage near to shore. We looked for a mooring.

Weaving in and out of the lanes of boats we asked advice. 'You'll have to double moor,' said one authoritative yachtie, sipping his third G&T. 'That mooring has only one boat on. That's OK,' he assured, waving a magnanimous hand. Ill at ease we awkwardly started to tie up. There was no one aboard the boat already moored. Thank goodness we were spending the evening with A and H. Such dormitory proximity had shades of Gairlochy on the Canal.

A large ostentatious plastic craft swung into line with our stern. 'That's my boat!' the equally large ostentatious female skipper hollered, indicating the boat already moored on the other side. 'And so is this. This is my mooring. Move off!' It was obvious that this Amazon would brook no interference, despite the technical fact that no one 'owns' HIDB moorings. We untied and skulked over to *Moonshine of Kip* and asked permission to raft on for the night. They were not pleased; but they were gentlemanly and ladylike in response to our pathetic room-at-the-inn situation. Rafting one boat on to another takes ages. After tying bow and stern ropes and fitting fenders exactly right, critical is the securing of the spring rope which ensures no free parallel movement.

It had taken us two hours to get *Anassa* parked. A was at the slipway with the car. 'You were having troubles?' He'd been watching us with the binoculars in the Sound even before we had rounded Calve Island. Like all retired seadogs his kennel is on a prime site overlooking the bay and the Sound. 'Come on, your dinner's ready.'

I could tell that A was fired up by our adventure. After dinner out came the old charts, the 1960s edition of the Clyde Cruising Club Sailing Directions bound in salt-stained covers with overlaid additional pilotage notes annotated in A's neat draughtsman's hand, his 1956 watercolour illustrated log of the West Coast Voyage of the *Camilla*, a yacht of *Anassa*'s size.

A belongs to the era of the Captain's inclination and fascination. The Scottish Council for Physical Recreation was founded in the early 1950s. It offered climbing and skiing instruction at Glenmore Lodge in the Cairngorms initially. *Camilla* became involved in SCPR's day sailing courses on the Clyde set up by Jock Kerr-Hunter, the moving spirit behind the scheme which soon offered West Coast cruising with larger boats. The scheme enabled A to move on to *La Goleta*, a 54-foot Bermudan Staysail Schooner accommodating seven crew. *Zuleika, Owl, Saionara*, and *Faireag* made up some of the first few of the fleet sponsored by SCPR. The 'crews' were for the most part desk-bound townies who, without fail, had the experience of their lives.

Enclosed some leaflets which will help a wee bit in giving you an idea
of holiday. It suits the young in mind and depends a lot on what you
make it. If you want a totally different life from normal and are
prepared to adjust then I can recommend this holiday. It certainly is

enjoyed by those who enjoy it – sounds Irish that one – but over half
are repeats (some for 4 or 5 years) so it canna be sae bad.

Thus responded one characterful skipper to an inquiry. The holidays became very successful and were based in Tobermory.

Islaborg, in due course, completed the list of boats owned by A, whose names will long be remembered by many 'crew'. Not only did A go to magical secret anchorages at the end of each day but he went there and returned safely. His regulars came back year after year. One of them was H – who stayed. H added the feminine touch to below decks decor and replaced fry-ups and beans on toast with epicurean cuisine laced with talk of local flora and fauna, sea life and history for boat guests. SCPR had fulfilled its aim of launching people into the world of cruising.

Was I trying to capture on *Anassa* something that I had been too young to participate in all those years back? Maybe, after all, I yearned as much for the days of unproscribed initiative and freedom as did the Captain.

We slept back aboard Anassa, the rafting was successful but a weather eye was necessary. Next morning was 'big shop' day and where better than Tobermory? Gone are the days of fruit and vegetable-less island stores. Tobermory has not only a supermarket but local shops that sell everything from an anchor to a pin, an excellent bakery – *pain au chocolat!* – with local milk, cheeses and vegetables, a fish shop and smokery. The Isle of Mull Pottery and the Isle of Mull Silver Shop along with the Frock Shop were reluctantly skirted past.

Mull has two ports. The newer one is at Craignure nearer to Oban, which has its own monster ferry several times daily packed with local vehicles. In the summer season tourist cars and buses for Iona vie for spaces with agricultural, timber, fuel and service transport. Practically all goods for Tobermory now come in this ferry and are then conveyed twenty miles overland on one of the worst roads on Mull. Traditionally and historically Tobermory is the capital of the island, but the shift in communication link is slowly but surely eroding its identity. Will it become a brightly painted picture postcard Heritage Port, where tourists will wander along Main Street and wonder at the rusting rings on the rotting pier that no longer links the outlying islands of Coll and Tiree? Small communities survive against all economic odds. Neither island can implement the Health and Safety rules governing milk production for public consumption, so the only source of fresh milk comes from the dairy in Tobermory, three days a week in winter and every day save Thursday and Sunday in the summer, when *The Lord of the Isles* does the six-hour return trip from its home port of Oban calling in at Tobermory in both directions. New timetabling of late has quietly reduced the number of times *Loti* has called at Tobermory. The writing is on the pier planks.

In the baker's window a very large glossily iced cake in the shape of the ferry caught my eye. It was to be auctioned at the end of the campaign to 'Save Our Link – Don't Let Islands Sink'.

> It is proposed by CalMac (Shipping Company) that from the summer of '98 ferry services between Tobermory and the islands of Coll and Tiree will cease. At once, an essential social and economic link that has existed for generations will be cut and we will become entirely isolated from our neighbouring islands. This closure is proposed not because facilities are degenerating or unsafe, not because the route is unviable or unused, but because £15 million of public money has been spent on a ferry which is too big to berth at Tobermory pier.

The campaign has not been successful and *Loti* sails wide out in the Sound full steam ahead from Oban to Coll and Tiree without the irritation and, much more relevant, time-wasting detour into Tobermory. 'She' is laden with 'Glasgow bread' (i.e., spun polystyrene) and UHT milk.

Collachs cleverly changed the name of *The Lord of the Isles* to *Loti*. Now 'he' can become a real boat, androgynised. But what of the new monster ferry being built? Will it have a gilded or gelded name?

Diesel and water was kindly ferried by A to the slipway for us. At least eight inflatables from yachts moored in the bay lay high and dry, all shades of grey, on the rocky edge of the slipway. Like basking seals at all angles waiting for the tide to lift them off. A tells the story of the reaction to the first rubber dinghy that came to the island in the '60s.

'I'd seen them before, of course. But the old *bodachs* standing around the phenomenon were bemused. Eventually the oldest and canniest said, 'I'd rather go to sea in a MacIntosh coat.'

The Captain whooped with joy. He had been meaning to identify our rubber dinghy ever since the Canal. Ordinarily somewhere on the bow or stern it should say 'Tender to *Anassa*'. He went off straight away to get a thick marker pen from Brown's Ironmongers and Wine Merchants on Main Street.

Goodbye, A and H. I hope we live up to your expectations and our own in the weeks still ahead aboard *Anassa*. I know the dinghy will have a name at last. 'MacIntosh Coat to *Anassa*'. Now is that male or female?

Ardnamurchan

Leaving the clamjamfry of Tobermory Bay, its flurry of sailing dinghies competing in and around the mooring, was liberating. 'God is Love' painted on the harbour entrance rock wished us well. The Captain, hoping for good sailing as ever, doffs his cap.

'There *is* a God!' he jubilates as a vanguard of guillemots leads us up the Sound of Mull, a following wind filling the sails. The tide is pushing us out to the headland of Ardnamurchan and the open sea. White scuddy meringue clouds on an overhead platter of new washed blue race *Anassa* to the lighthouse. The long, scarred mountainous finger of Ardnamurchan that captured Daniell with such dramatic humour spears to starboard. *Anassa* is so alive! If we have got it right, the tide pushing us out will meet the incoming tide coming up the Passage of Tiree which will take us flying northwards. A warned us of the potential bigness of the seas as we rounded Ardnamurchan Point. He was right. But instead of retreating to the galley for culinary displacement activity I exult in the roller-coaster troughs. Every monster of the deep would be far below in the seabed calms. The following sea is strong but has a benign strength. We make 6½ knots! *Anassa* is moving! The sails thwack, the bow wash frills and froths and sparkles. Our penetration of the sea is surface and slicing and glancing. The Captain's brown eyes are turning sea-dog blue. After days of slow Canal gliding and windless, limp-sailed motoring leading us to the failure-ridden attempt on Loch Etive and our increasing awareness

of being very behind on the schedule worked out at winter red-wined tables, our spontaneous, immediately shared excitement at such speed is as pure as the driven waves. The Captain wants to increase propulsion to maximise the tide. He cranks the engine alive. We are soon doing 8 knots! We can't hear each other speak. I take the wildflowers, the herb garden and sprouting seeds down from the doghouse roof to shelter behind the cabin door. This is serious sailing I tell them. I want you for later, at the end of this brilliant day, unshredded.

South-west to stern, the island lies flat as a board and quite unaware of our celebratory existence. I have a momentary feeling of betrayal and guilt. The changing, eliding silhouettes of the Small Isles, Cuillins of Skye beyond, Blaven and the Red Cuillins nearer, all with a pale lime-yellow backdrop sky, look like blue-grey icebergs floating south. Another limelight glances on the distant serrated

Rounding Ardnamurchan
(56° 42′N 6° 17′W)
27 Fathoms

hills of the Cuillins. We truly do fly northwards, starboard past Portuairk and bright green Sanna Bay, Grigadale Port, Faskadale, Kilmory, Ockle. And Swordle at the end of the road of Ardnamurchan. Isolated places all permanently thralled to the witnessing of a day sliding magnificently westwards to its ending whether in storm or calm or fog or, as today, Force 5, visibility clear.

Maybe I am a deep-sea mariner when rock and sandbars are where they should be. Deep down with all the other horrors but close to the land. I let my body go with the motion of the ship, feet far enough apart to roll on the ball of each foot, a hand gripping the doghouse roof rail. I've learned over years of regular island ferry crossings not to fight the movement. To exult in it. It is sensual, swooning and arresting in turn. It is going with the flow, truly. When young, seasickness as with carsickness was part of the inevitable agony of

travel. The condition was born of fear and never addressed, for I was a child. It is a natural reaction to such outrageous imbalance. We are, after all, terrestrial beings.

The Fife and Forfar Yeomanry consisting predominantly of farm workers sailed from Liverpool in 1900 on board ss *Cymric*, a White Star liner requisitioned to take troops to fight in the Boer War in South Africa. So did their horses, all six hundred of them, stabled between decks. Corporal Charles Hunter from Cupar recorded in a notebook, amongst many other fascinating items, that on the voyage it daily took four or five men to peel 2 tons of potatoes for men and horses during the several weeks it took to get to their destination. He regularly went below decks beyond the call of duty to calm the tethered horses, amongst them his own horse, Bowhill. The horses were never off their feet from the time they left Cupar. The heat in the stables was unbearable, 97–110 degrees. Several of the men contracted 'stable throat'. Only officers' horses were groomed. But even those 'we saw the bones of them.'

Before the Canaries the human death toll starts. 'Death of Ogilvie. Funeral at one o'clock. First of us to die. Engines of boat don't stop.' It was not only men that died; it was horses and several of those due to the motion of the ship. Horses, like humans, can get seasick unto death. Bowhill survived, as did Corporal Hunter. The Corporal's notebook is in the National Library of Scotland.

Travelling with a carsick dog as well as a child or two is a nightmare second only to one's own *mal de voiture*. As for cats in baskets … Must be even worse with budgies but maybe not. Parrots are associated with pirates' cabins and images of the sea. Birds are familiar with the swoops and arrests of flight, after all. It must be when they are land bound, chained to a perch, that parrots get sick.

I have great faith in pressure point wristbands. Faith is the operative word. The Icelandic fishermen's tip of nibbles of apple and brown bread works. As does the judicious sip or two of brandy and the ballast of a large bowl of porridge, tea and toast at the start of the day. Pills have me dopily floating; that's all right as a big ship's passenger but not for me aboard *Anassa*.

But no matter which placebo is sworn by, the most valuable remedy is that of mental preparation based on enjoying, exulting in the experience. This is a tricky art to learn; so many imponderables can twist the gut of confidence with one rogue wave of tension or imbalance. A 'heavy' night before sailing, letting oneself get too cold and wet on deck, sustaining conversational chit-chat to the point of competitive bravado when every loop of one's intestine is starting to quease in warning knots, bending down for that fallen spoon or book, the smell of greasy cooking, and absolutely most fatal of all, another's vomit. At any of these trigger points I immediately lie down wrapped warm in a rug and think myself into the wombed state of the embryo that sways and lurches with the movement of its mother host. Eventually the up, down, sideways rhythmic roll lulls and soothes. The hand of Mother Sea rocks the cradle. The timing of this escape route is critical. If misjudged, the ensuing fight is unto death. A watery death. For surely, there is no more suicidal condition than seasickness once vomiting occurs. The French *mal de mer* has too gentle and poetic a nuance for such a physical and mental degradation. They, of course, have only one open coastline and have never been viewed as a maritime nation.

As if to add insult to injury, once voided the stomach is clawed and torn and scarified as if by a demented wild beast intent on dragging one's very bowels up through one's ruptured throat. Perhaps that is the worst sea monster of all.

Adolphe Blanqui, writing in 1823, has an interesting comment on seasickness. He believed our physical and mental sensibilities in relation to the sea were different from those of our ancient ancestors, who never list seasickness as one of man's infirmities.

It is a serious (disability) for us, who are not as simple as our forefathers, and it certainly has an important place in the history of the traveller's tribulations. As soon as land is out of sight, joy and movement vanish from the ship; all conversations are suddenly broken off, and the rosiest faces abruptly lose colour and take on a ghastly greenish complexion. One often sees women stretched out on deck in a state of total dejection, unaware of everything that goes on around them … Everyone seems to withdraw into himself.

[*Voyage d'un jeune Français en Angleterre et en Ecosse*]

Anassa is not out of sight of land, but she is full of 'joy and movement'. Sparkling rain squalls do not diminish but enhance the effervescence of our progression up the coast. White skelfs of sails like sloping exclamation marks emphasise the way ahead. These are big boys soon disappearing from sight, making for the evening yachtie culture of Isle Ornsay on Skye, where loud drinks and four-course dinners await their land-based culture ashore.

The lightship *Fingal*, coming from Eigg to port, powers a bore of wake across our bows as she heads for her homeland harbour of Oban. A helicopter perched aft, the great cranes to pull up the lightbuoys for inspection and servicing for'ard. A familiar of the western seaboard for twenty or more years she does her tour of maintenance with the regularity of an old friend's mindfulness. All lighthouses around the coast of Britain are now automated. *Fingal* carries on the traditional triangular relationship of lights and boats and men, somehow, with a human touch despite the lightbuoys being automated too. Lighthouses are mostly land based and lesser in number than the hundreds of lightbuoys that swing and tug at the mercy of tides and storms. *Fingal* is of their element.

We are so close to this wise old mother ship that I like to think she wants to say 'Ahoy' to our history. But the Captain does not believe in using the radio for 'chatter'. 'Bloody yachties use it all the time, taking up channel space to ask each other if they've got any gin left. Coastguards get furious.' Au revoir, *Fingal*.

Loch Ailort

The Captain was getting tetchy. Our jubilant 6½ knots was not surfing the tide any longer. We were now punching against the tide. Enticing Eilean Shona beckoned from the mouth of Loch Moidart. 'No use,' said the Captain, 'tide not right.' Once again it all depends on the tide … It is raining.

By 10pm we are just coming up to Goat Island off Loch Ailort. The loch has a reputation for strong winds helter skeltering down the slopes of Am Falachan. And tonight is the night. Opposite dimming Roshven House, snuck back into a darkening wood, there is token shelter in the bay from a small bluff. A single other yacht is already anchored, hatches battened down, her fixed mizzen sail keeping her bow into the increasingly boisterous offshore wind. *Meltemi*, our neighbour for the night, rides steady. Will we?

Anchoring is a forgotten art, says Colin Jones in *Cruiser Management (Helmsman Guides)*. Up till now we have had benign enough conditions to practise this art. Tonight there is a wild conspiracy in the air. Always a tense and time-consuming exercise conditioned by so many factors – depth, seabed conformation, tidal movement, possible river outflow, position of already anchored boats, and wind direction. Our routine has equably evolved where I steer, the Captain ordering from the bow, anchor poised in his brawny arms for its snaking descent to dig into sand or mud and clinch our security. I have the engine at its lowest revs waiting for the order 'Neutral!' The final slow glide is engineless. I am also, at this point, hand on tiller, stretching and ducking into the cabin to read and bawl out the echo sounder readings. A couple of reconnoitring circles usually suffices. 'Anchor away,' the Captain will formally announce. (He is a stickler for nautical protocol. 'Coming aboard,' he'll call with serious import from the dinghy after some fishing or shore foray on his own. Seems daft to me when I am the only person to hear. I reply, 'Aye, Aye, Captain!' and the ritual is completed to his satisfaction.)

'Aye, Aye, Captain!' I shout to the four winds that whip the words out to sea. When the anchor touches the seabed he will instruct by uplifted hand for the engine to be put into reverse. Ideally this movement should be straight downwind for the anchor chain to be laid along the seabed letting the anchor bite further in with a lateral pull. Anchors are laid not dropped. This final copybook activity is proving nigh impossible to achieve. It was as though the winds of the mountains were challenging us and saying, 'You thought the sea and its tides and currents were the final unconquerable element. Listen to *us!*' Every time I manage to get *Anassa* in line and above the patch of lightness indicating sand below, the wind flings her powerless bow round. It is essential that we compensate for the eventuality of the wind changing direction in the night not only to estimate where she might end up on the 150-foot length of chain shorewards but also in relation to *Meltemi*. Thanks to her mizzen her position will probably remain static. *Anassa* without such an aid could whirl and swirl like a 180-degree dervish the radius of the anchor chain.

We lined up the firefly lights of a caravan in amongst trees as a shore mark. Conveniently it turned out that the inhabitants were having an all-night party or the toddler couldn't sleep without a light being left on. I thought of the big yachts at Isle Ornsay slumbering by now on programmed computered anchors that of their own accord activate the engine to face the boat into the variability of any wind direction, captains and crews in the arms of Morpheus, their bellies quietly burping langoustine, caviar and cream juices in time to the soft thrum of generators. I thought of the captain and crew of the *Fingal* moored at Oban. They've been to the pictures, now walking back via the pub to the fish and chip shop, some to go home to a broad bed, some to snug into their on-duty bunk, the late-night movie on a portable TV at their feet.

A hasty fry-up supper that used up the last of the Greasy Joe supplies lies heavy on our hearts and consciences. Such breakfast food of the gods must only be consumed on special, ritually pure occasions. Sundays are preferred by the gods and are therefore propitious. It is Saturday night. Ominously stressed clunks come from the anchor chain, the rigging howls. We take anchor watch in turns, the little light on shore winking fixed reassurance.

The dawn came sunny. *Anassa* slewed less dramatically on an anchor that had not moved an inch all night, dappled sun patterns shifted back and forth within the cabin. The demon winds of Am Falachan were turning their backs on us. They had had their fun with the sailors; it was time to search out the hillwalkers.

The calm after the storm. The sleeping bags are aired over the boom, washing flaps from the rails. We sit on deck not really missing the Greasy Joe breakfast. We decide it is Monday. There is lots of fruit and we feel as clean as the wind-cleansed landscape. *Meltemi* is gone and we are left alone. I imagine the heyday of Roshven House. This time of year there would be at least one schooner like the *Witch* anchored where we were; and also a steam motor cruiser disembarking guests by rowboat to the boathouse where a pony and trap would transport the ladies to the Big House, while the men stayed behind to share a dram or two with the host, his gamekeeper and gillies before loading guns and telescopes and wicker baskets onto the backs of long-maned Highland garrons that, come the end of the day, would be draped with 12-pointer Stag Royals. The Highland Holiday that Queen Victoria so popularised. The Monarch of the Glen Shooting Party. Perhaps Landseer was there with his sketch-book, canvas and paints. The ladies would be thrilled and ask for advice on watercolour technique when he crossed the lawn.

But the lady of the house would not have been in awe of him should he have called, for she knew him and had had lessons from him in London as a younger woman. Jemima Blackburn was one of the foremost Victorian illustrators and watercolourists of her time. She and her husband Hugh bought Roshven Estate in 1854 and began the improvements to which in no small way her remuneration from illustration commissions contributed. She had her own special projects. On hearing that the people were held to ransom by traders on account of their isolation, she took it upon herself to buy goods, some the likes of which had never been seen in Loch Ailort, at cost in Glasgow and shipped once a week, which she then sold to locals without commission. Many of her watercolours depict the day-to-day life of the Estate and are an intimate record of its heyday.

The boat house is in ruinous condition like a rotted molar at the loch edge. The Big House has a great silent look about it. I want to believe its hallway walls still sprout 12-point antlers atop solemn staring-eyed stuffed stag heads, fish mounted on mahogany plaques longer than the angler's sideways stretched arms, eagles and owls dusty-feathered in glass cases, the game book lying open on top of the oak chest with the double page copperplate list of the last day's 'bag'. Moth-eaten plaid carpet. Little verdigreed silver bell by the hand crank telephone that no maid will ring for tea, great round gong with pigskin-padded stick that no butler will brassily resonate for dinner.

'Time to get shipshape.' The Captain was back on duty. Bad weather can leave a boat messy and untidy. There is no time for the finer points of domesticity. As usual he had 'on deck' duties. The dinghy had to be baled and, of course, he had to test its outboard in case water had got into the carburettor.

I enjoyed pottering on *Anassa* on my own and didn't mind when the ubiquitous West Coast drizzle beaded the varnished teak of the cockpit. I'd got the bags and washing in in time. The mizzen flag now flapped wetly on its own. Tidying and stowing away was not a chore. It was lovely sitting alone in the small world of *Anassa* that had been my home for over a fortnight and would be for several weeks yet. Everything within hand's reach and me outwith anyone's reach. The cabin rocked and creaked gently, a vestige of the night's eerie wind toying with the bow. Terns screeched somewhere far away to land.

I remember the house of tea-chest walls I made in the copper beech tree as a child; the numerous, each one individual, nomad tents I designed with the wooden clothes horse as a frame draped in sheets and carpets at the furthest end of the garden from the house. It was not entirely the gender of nest-building expressing itself; it was my very own place, away from parents, their house, their rooms, their rules. It was my own space that I had created for myself. No obligations, no expectations from others. Hiding away, maybe. But like an anchorite fixed, not just to the private place, but, more importantly, within one's own ease. Anchorite, anchor.

I think I could live like this on my own for ever. Each day moving on, but taking the familiar nomad's tent of sail with me, lockers full of fine food and wine, books on the porthole shelf and the womb rock of sleep at day's ending. Unfortunately, I don't have the strength to hand crank the engine and I need the Captain to anchor.

'Coming aboard!' The Captain is back. He has decided to anchor *Anassa* in the lee of Goat Island (Eilean nan Gobhar) for the night. 'The weather is settled. The sunset will be stunning from its highest points.'

As we motor over I tell him of my musings on anchors and homes and solitude. As ever he has an addendum.

'Yes, yes, interesting symbols, especially the anchor. It has both desirable and undesirable connotations, you know.'

'Well, our CQR held ground very desirably last night in very testing circumstance,' I volunteered, defensively. The Captain was in sage mode, however, and was not interested in practical conversation.

'Its symbol goes beyond seafaring circles. Homes, jobs, families and numerous other familiarities can be figurative anchors. Houses and universal mortgages in particular.' I sensed this man was affirming something hard won and dearly held.

'It is interesting that you have linked the anchor and the home,' he continued. 'Kahlil Gibran in *The Prophet* trips the anchor memorably on the house as image of entrapment when he says: "But you, children of space, you restless in rest, you shall not be trapped or tamed. Your house shall not be an anchor but a mast." Because you can see it from afar and come back to it, you see? It is not a possession that locks you in. Did you know that the very last link of anchor chain attached at the boat end, the "possession" end, is called the "bitter end". Think on't.'

Perchance to dream, we 'children of space' might live on *Anassa* for ever, bitter end or not. Is this what he is saying?

As though to leave *Anassa* alone to ponder in her wisdom this possibility, we took off in the dinghy to explore further up Loch Ailort. We knew its north shore well, having spent many crazy happy times with our old weekending bothy crowd at Penmeanach – Peenie Meenie – having walked in from Polnish on the Mallaig road, some of us canoeing over from Glen Uig. The children and dogs travelling the land route with the less adventurous adults. Sometimes the children reluctant on the trek but bursting out in 'over-the-hills-and-far-away' energy once the old crofthouse was reached, rucksacks offloaded and the cry for driftwood and fallen branches from the birch woods hollered. Late at night there were midnight swims and some hardy souls slept on the beach, waking to the shiver of dawn and happy to get back to the snoring bothy and brew up the first Lapsang Souchong of the day.

We had to retread old ground. It happens as sure as the going down of the sun when one gets older.

With a little distaste we saw from the dinghy that someone was at the bothy. 'A bit early,' said the Captain in disgust. 'In our day we would be on the hill till the last of the light.'

Dragging the dinghy up above the tideline we saw the tips of great crops of large purple-blue mussels clinging to rocks that would soon be accessible as the tide lowered. We wandered up to the bothy, reminiscing. Two youngish men sat outside, one reading a book entitled *Emotional Intelligence*. This took us somewhat aback. We took bird and fungi books with us on those halcyon days. We felt it encumbent to detail our Penmeanach pedigree. This did not seem to interest them. Persisting in our mission we went through the door to the stone-walled hall of our youthful selves and families. Two young canoeists were divvying up rice and something. It was a halting conversation with them, too.

I begin to notice as I get older that younger people are not really interested in what I have to say. And no wonder, you might say. But I truly believe, surely by now, I have less to say but what there is, is of greater value. I have to believe that. Don't they want to hear about the past of this place? Those days so important to us. Are we but shadows in the landscape? Were we being patronising telling our old bothying tales? We were three isolated groups. We thinking to give, the other two groups unknown to each other till the present time, unable to take. It was like going into a class of children where peer children from another school have been invited by well-meaning staff to share the experience of a visiting author. The two sets of children more intent on sussing each other out, unable to relax and get involved in the creative exchange of question and answer lest they expose or make fools of themselves. Somewhat disappointed we left for the mussels. There was almost a hint that the mussels belonged to them. Well, if they did, they would have needed a pantechnicon to garner them all. 'Didn't even offer us a cup of tea. Not old style bothyers,' grumbled the Captain, as we filled polybags with mussels, aware of being watched on 'their' shore.

MacIntosh Coat to Anassa was low in the water as we made for home. Our floating Peenie Meenie. Our mast. We headed into a brisk wind, spray coming over the blunt, bouncing, rubbery bow. My rucksack of sketching materials hastily clad in a black dustbin liner.

And then the outboard engine choked dead. The dinghy backed inexorably to the shore and the watching bothyers. The Captain rowed hard to make way to get depth and consequent time to examine the Seagull. It had to be electrics or fuel starvation, he said. The wind played with *MacIntosh Coat to Anassa* like a waterborne leaf. Exposed, we were now the fools. Not a lifejacket between us, caught out by the fickleness of fjord conditions where the wind was a playground of whoops and swoops. I didn't care about the lifejackets. My concern was for the rucksack of sketching materials. Right at the start of the voyage the Captain had made a float attachment to the rucksack should the worst happen. I was preparing myself for water-colours *con mare* that would be washed up on the Penmeanach shore for the unbothyers to add to their possessions and my humiliation.

It was my turn to row. Quite ineffectually, but the Captain found the fuel pipe disconnection and we were back to forward movement, our backs proud to the inhospitable shore, our mast beckoning us to safety and ethical space.

· The Mackerel Thieves ·

The sunset was stunning. As were the mussels stewed on the beach driftwood fire on Goat Island. Old Tobermory bread dunked in white wine and herb water took on a new lease of life. As did we. Climbing to the top of the island for the last of the sunset over Eigg, Rum peaked and silhouetted beyond, we sat on the rampart remains of the first vitrified fort I have seen. The burnt fused lumps of small stones, the stones more ancient than the ancients who configured them for protective walls, were like a contemporary raku potter's creation. I felt their rough history, trailing my fingers over gritty bumps and blisters. My history, urban bothyers and cruddy old Seagull engines burnt up in a conflagration of irrelevance. I looked down to *Anassa*'s mast. Another quite unpredicted day was over.

Loch Moidart

The tide was right to enter Loch Moidart. A close-hauled jib scudded us easily back the way we had come a couple of days previously. The island of Eigg had a different profile to starboard. A dozing crocodile, hopefully an indicator of benign weather. The entrance to Loch Moidart is very detailed and downright dangerous when exiting if a south-westerly blows. We could ill afford to be trapped; we wanted to achieve our clutch of fjordings. The Captain will not listen to the Shipping Forecast on Radio 4. Irrelevant, he says, frowning his dark frown.

Living on the island it was my meteorological bible, Malin my sea plot. 'And now the Shipping Forecast issued by the Met Office …' The slow anticipation as the coastal areas starting 'Viking, Forties …' crept anti-clockwise round Britain. 'Rockall, *Malin*, Hebrides …' How many black winter late-night and early-morning vigils were held round the wireless in the kitchen, bags packed by the door for the mainland visit? Would the boat call or not? Would the storm pass or rage for days? Would return be possible when planned? In those days there was no CalMac Disrupt Line to inform of cancelled services. No Marinecall, Weathercall or MetFax Marine. No mobile phones shackled to lanyards. Just the wireless and Mrs Ferguson in the telephone exchange on the next island who would know when and if the boat had called there. Over the howling dark ether the calm, intimately caring voice of the radio announcer, deep in the night-time bowels of Shepherds Bush, read his broadcast always commencing with 'Good evening, Gentlemen,' the gentle emphasis on the second word.

Since the first broadcasts in 1924 which introduced a town and rural population to the mysterious coded language of the Shipping Forecast, the sea-wrapped one-ness of our Sceptered Isle belonged to everyone, not just those who made a living from the sea. One wonders how much of a role the daily transmissions of the Shipping Forecast played in the sense of nationhood that grew strong as the storm clouds gathered over Europe. Was it a political device as well as an information service for those in peril at sea? Surely not. The announcer wore a bow tie and evening dress. Such sartorial rig is not the outfit of a politician. Or dictator.

The necklace of names, some familiar, some historical, some dramatically remote, all rhythmically threaded, create a protective chain of assurance and identity. Landlubbers in deepest Leeds, Manchester and Birmingham stop what they are doing and drift with the roundel of magical words, deep seas swelling within them.

Many artists, writers, poets, photographers have been attracted to the image. The sea swell of Seamus Heaney's poem; the photographer Mark Power, non-chauvinistic, widening the circle to include the other nations and cultures that edge 'our' seaboard.

The Met Office was established as the Meteorological Department of the Board of Trade in 1854 with Captain Robert Fitzroy at the helm. Previous helmsmanship included a tour of duty with Darwin on HMS *Beagle* between 1832 and 1835. Fitzroy inherited the limited method of gale warning system which consisted of black canvas cones hoisted at coastguard stations on receipt of a warning telegram. The point hoisted upward indicated a gale from the north, downwards from the south. Using the new invention of electric telegraph, Fitzroy introduced the first British storm warning service for shipping in 1861; by 1911 gale warnings were broadcast regularly for North Atlantic and coastal waters. In 1924 areas were broadly defined. Broadcasting was suspended during the Second World War. In 1949 the plotted chart of the sea area names appeared. There has been little change in fifty years. Viking now cedes inland to North and South Utsire. Trafalgar added on below Finisterre.

Only recently have insidious changes crept into one of Britannia's well-loved institutions. Gone is the personal touch. Sailors are no longer wished 'Goodnight and good sailing, gentlemen' at midnight's end. Possibly in deference to female trawler captains and Cross Atlantic singlehanded viragos. Broadcast times are reducing and changing channels. The rich tapestry of Radio 4 will soon, I fear, lose the pattern of sound strands, repeated, but always different, that halt the immediate and stretch the mind and imagination to far sea horizons in the midst of pedestrian, domestic activity.

I had thought my voyage on *Anassa* would give me the opportunity to say farewell *in situ*, so to speak, in a practical as well as sentimental way. I had taken my little kitchen radio cassette for the purpose. It was very difficult to get any signal on account of the everpresent headlands and hills. And doubly, trebly frustrating when the Captain showed not the least bit concern.

'Your island was in the *Atlantic*,' the Captain reminded me, equally frustrated at my fussing and knob-twiddling. 'We are, remember, for the most part in inland sea lochs that make their own weather. Remember Roshven. The land and its habitual relationship with the tide is what we should be concerned with.' The tide. Again. There was no getting away from it.

'This is our best indicator of bad weather.' He tapped the barometer. 'When that needle keeps going down, everyone but everyone, whether in deep sea or in close coastal waters is in for trouble, *real* trouble.' I could almost see the red, spotted bandana coming out and being tied round his neck.

'Do you want to forget the fjords and go out into the Atlantic? You'll hear your blessed Shipping Forecast there.' I did not. I'd wait till I got to my new mainland home deep in the hills and be like a Brummie.

Castle Tioram is so well protected by the narrow entrance to Loch Moidart. The apparently continuous coastline hides the entrance. It is only the pilot book that says it is there. Loch Moidart is a mini fjord and we enter it, successfully anchoring off Eilean Shona jetty, the Castle rearing opposite on a shingle spit. The 'dry castle' in translation. Dry because no great seas will ever get to it? Like a pearl in an oyster is its hidden location. If it was 'dry' for want of well water within its walls, there was no problem with supplies on the landward side. It was raining again.

I ask to be landed at the little sandy beach at its foot, the Captain dinghying to the real shore. I visited this ruin by land many years previously. My daughter's piano teacher in Fort William had a thing, and a caravan, about its environs. She had invited the family down for a Sunday outing. I remember taking an educational attitude to the situation. Her older brother (my daughter's, not the piano teacher's) reluctantly but politely toured the site eager to get back to the sanctuary of his motorcross magazines in the car. My daughter, the more confused child of '60s parents, looked hopelessly through seaward shells of windows with roofless sky above, wishing she had the equivalent insouciance that would also take her away from this artificial family exercise. I think that is when she decided not to take an interest in castellated history or piano lessons any more.

It was liberating to land on the shingle on my own and see the Castle for the first time, untrammelled. The Captain had tidal things to do with the dinghy.

I come from the sea like Venus reborn but with sagging mildly militant breasts. I pretend the Castle is inhabited. Will they let me in? Its domestic importance is easy to discern once inside the roofless walls. The tourist plaque on the landward side of the causeway further illustrates this. No warring or defensive activities are depicted. Why couldn't that family outing, all those years ago, have been as peaceable? By osmosis, if nothing else.

When I meet up with the Captain we walk a long 'just half an hour' to Acharacle for supplies. Greasy Joe needs feeding. We make the classic mistake of not casing the joint and, like desert starved rats, hit the mini supermarket on first sighting. Later, further along the village, we find a little Home Bakery full of condimental jam-jars and ciabatta olive bread.

The village is abuzz with the latest news. Castle Tiorem is for sale. £120,000, they say. The owners are descendants of Clanranald MacDonalds who built the Castle in 1351. A Los Angeles lawyer, Wiseman MacDonald, bought it in the early '20s of this century. I hope there is a wise man in the present generation of Californian MacDonalds who are now selling it and will take heed of the current mood in Scotland in relation to land ownership. No other country in Europe still has such feudal land tenure laws. A landowner can sell to the highest – or lowest – bidder without any obligation to protect national or cultural identity. Why, oh why, does Scotland let this happen? The French, our old allies, can't believe it. We are as backward as Latin America, they say.

The selling agents specialise in island properties. They have had 'several offers' already. Castle Tiorem comprises the 'island'.

Like a timely guiding light, only the previous week the lengthy, hard-won fight of the people of Eigg to buy their own island after years of recurring disruptive change of ownership, was joyously celebrated. Previous landlords of the island, cavalier for the most part, steeped in the mores of Queen Victoria's antlered Highlands, tried to sustain a dated utopia. The time capsule had to burst. As it did in Assynt where the crofters bought the Estate on which their family crofts had been worked from time immemorial. They became their own landlord, securing the traditional use of, and attitude to, the land as had their forefathers. They, forced to struggle on small units, developed a best practice rotation of the land's limited resources and diversified into other forms of income generation that is now held as a socio-agricultural exemplar.

There is an easing of Government attitude to part-funding such community buy-outs. The old Highlands and Islands Development Board set up in 1975 had a primary social remit to help stem endemic emigration. It had no powers to buy property for the benefit of the people. But things are changing. The locals in Acharacle, fired with Eigg's success in creating the Isle of Eigg Heritage Trust in partnership with Highland Regional Council and Scottish Wildlife Trust, already talk of a community bid for 'their' Castle. It was a tourist, a regular summer swallow, who told us all this, her eyes shiny with identification. Community ownership can only be viable if the community is viable. Financial consideration is not the main criterion for this viability. The most important ingredient is the respect for consensus and integrity; both leavened further with the ability to have an overview collectively and not let individual dogmas and obsessions fragment the initial concept and commitment. I greatly admire the individuals who make up these communities, let alone the communities themselves. One rotten apple in the box can rot the rest very quickly.

Walking back through Acharacle with our rucksacks full of goodies there was a brilliant yellow-green field of mown grass husbanded into rounded rucks of tawny hay. A strip of oats trembled a feathered blue-green in the light breeze. Drills of white flowering potatoes cried out for butter and chopped chives on a hot plate. I realised I missed my vegetable garden. The sacrifice of a summer on a boat. The mini market had had tired tatties and leathery carrots. 'Well, you can't have everything,' chided the Captain, who might be a secret Pot Noodle man, I think. We diverted to the little Telford kirk above the road westwards to Loch Moidart. There were summer flowers in vases on the deep-set window sills. A notice said 'Please take your *Life and Work* from the back pew.' I did. There were a lot of them; the magazines looked interesting. It was not until I got back to *Anassa* that I noticed the biroed handwritten name of a parishioner on the top left-hand corner of the front cover. 'You are such a literal person,' the Captain guffawed. It still hangs heavy on me that theft.

The Storm

We had enjoyed our perambulations on shore. But the sea called, where there are no signposts that direct the way or say 'Private. Keep Out.' The last open territory where one can wander at will. Weather permitting.

It was good to be back in the oil-lit cabin, poring over the charts for the next day's passage to Arisaig, replete with tagliatelle carbonara preceded by mussel bisque from Peenie Meenie with olive bread and followed by Acharacle goat's cheese and firm fresh peaches. All washed down by fine wine from the mini market. A cognac or two.

It was to be an 11am up-anchoring for the tide out. Bliss. A lie-in. We blow out the lamps. Lying in the dark there was no way of telling what the weather was like 'out there' so sheltered was the anchorage. The sibilant ripple of an occasional little wave along the length of *Anassa*'s hull, the call of an owl in the islanded wood of Riska, teak creaking on teak, single clunk of the anchor chain tweaked by an underwater eddy, drip-drip of rain on the doghouse roof, only the sentry awake in the Castle, the clink of his Claymore catching the wall as he stretches to put another branch on the fire, rubs his weary eyes. A deerhound yawning.

The rain had stopped by morning but a damp cloud hung over the night-soaked land, the sea dull grey watersilk. Whatever movement there was could be heard out beyond the entrance to the Loch. Faint, but there. I could not make out if it was a welcome or a warning. I saw the Captain tap the barometer.

The visibility got worse as we headed for the intricate exit of Loch Moidart. The wind was rising from the south. 'She'll fly to Arisaig in this,' whooped the Captain, tying the red, black-spotted bandana round his neck. On reaching the open sea the damp dank drizzle of Moidart was whipped away by a steely Force 6 to 7, the watersilk surface a cauldron of turbulence as the south-westerly wind impatiently forced the just turning slack tide into the Loch with no consideration for the narrowness of the opening. *Anassa* bucked and writhed. We could have turned back but the time taken to think the thought lost us the opportunity. We were right into the open sea. We were committed.

The jib goes up, then the mainsail. 'At last the wind is for us not against,' shouts the Captain over the thwack and crash of wind and wave. 'We're doing 6½ knots, surging 7, way over hull speed!' He is blue-eyed again. 'We're *planing* over the troughs!' The eyes are bluer.

This was the first time that I had been told to wear my safety harness. It should have made me feel more at ease. It didn't. I was very ill at ease. The green of fear was creeping up on me. White-knuckled I gripped the doghouse rail and tried to think sensuous flowing thoughts. I couldn't. It was critical that I held on tight, rigidly counterbalancing the slope of the deck. We were in a quartering sea, broaching to port, the water up to the gunwale as she heeled to starboard. The Captain tried to remind me of the 4-foot lead keel. Meant not a thing.

I will the south headland of Arisaig, dimly perceivable ahead when the rain blasts stop, to come nearer, nearer. To stern the haven of Moidart. Also a large fishing trawler, anchored in the lea of Acarsaid. Like a scene from an old Second World War black and white film, its dark grey bulk just discernible from the lighter grey headland behind, both edged with white-flecked waves.

I know *that* captain has listened to the Shipping Forecast.

I concentrate on a flock of guillemots – what are they doing out in such weather? – which look amazed as we flee past. A colossal seal rears its thick brown-coated head out of the water just feet away. I think it is a walrus so disoriented have I become. The sea so cold, so grey, so foreign. I am with Scott approaching

Antarctica. I am very cold and wet. A grey iceberg floating past would not be amazing.

There is no way I can retreat to culinary therapy. The doghouse door is shut. I do not like this. There is no womb to *Anassa*. I don't ask the Captain why this is so. I know deep down why.

And then the very thing this precaution was taken for happened. A breaking wave from port lashes over the doghouse. Next, an extreme starboard roll is accompanied by crashes and clatters from the cabin. The kettle is on my bunk, water everywhere, the books from the library shelf opposite are slurping back and forth in inches of bilge water. The open-fronted 'cool larders' at cabin deck level have spewed out gobbets of fruit and veg. In amongst the books, mangoes bash into tatties, tomatoes play water polo with oranges. Half-opened cheese and bacon have taken on a sickly suspended pallor. 'Leave them!' the Captain commands. 'Get pumping!' The lump of port water was too much for the cockpit drainers.

'But the books!'

'Bugger the books!!'

We take turns at the helm and pumping the bilges. I do not know which is worse. At the helm I strain every last ounce of my weight to port to bring *Anassa* to at least a half even keel. I honestly believe I can do it, if I really try. Equally, hand pumping the bilges, numb knuckles chafed on the cockpit facing, I know every drop of water must be pumped out or we will surely go down to Davy Jones's locker. Though if I could be assured of a hot toddy, a hot water bottle and a warm comfy linen-sheeted bed, I might consider letting it happen.

I start to panic about my notes and sketches under my bunk mattress.

'They might have slipped out!' I wail to the wind in the rigging. I have to climb down into the maelstrom of the cabin to find out. The notebooks and sketchbooks were intact in their sealed poly folders firmly jammed under the mattress. I salvage the books from the slushing diesel-streaked water to a higher closed locker until I get the opportunity to dry them out. Despite layers of clothing and wet-weather gear, every bit of my body is punched and hammered as I bounce between cabin fittings and the mast pillar support. Everything begins to look a bilious green in the blur of the wet oily detritus of *Anassa*'s bowels.

I catapult myself into the cockpit, grab the doghouse rail and look desperately to the still-distant rain-blinded headland of Arisaig. I will myself to fight the nausea. The Captain gives me the helm, seeing it is critical. By now I don't care what angle the boat is at. I'll do anything to get *Anassa* to port. Any port. My concentration is phenomenal. The Captain is in the cabin with the charts. The channel to the inner harbour of Arisaig winds through a labyrinth of rocks.

> Written instructions would only confuse, as the coast line is so broken up, and the rocks and islets are bewildering. The detail chart 2817 is the only sure guide, and it would be well to make this harbour for the first time at L.W., or soon after, when the reefs are showing.

> [*The Clyde Cruising Club Sailing Directions*]

Neil Gunn quotes the same extract in *Off in a Boat*. He and his wife ('the Crew') crossed from Eigg to Arisaig in identical conditions forty years ago. Just as my Captain rejoices in the plunging rolls and flying spray so did hers. ' "A pretty good boat, this of ours",' he shouts to 'the Crew' halfway to Arisaig, the engine racing as the propeller is lifted out of the sea, the bow smacking perilously low on the down side of the wave. 'She smiled, clearly at the stage of nearly believing it, but still with a certain pale reserved judgment.' The similarities are uncanny. Or is it just men and boats?

Our apprehensions of the 'labyrinth of rocks', the winding channel with notorious, seemingly unrelated perches marking the way were as well-founded as theirs. But then we were reading the same pilot book. What a revelation rounding the shelter of Rhubh Arisaig was the sighting of new large brightly painted perches, many more than before, easily followed in the rain drifts and dropping wind. Soaking sails were furled. The putter of the engine sweet music. Every nerve in my body twitched and flitched. I'd not relax until we were anchored.

The rain had stopped drifting. It was straightforward longitudinal stair-rodding. Everything, but everything was wet. Inside and out. Unbelievably the herbs and the sprouter wedged behind the cabin doors had survived. The wildflowers of Moidart looked a bit frayed.

Why we went ashore, soaked to a soaking Arisaig, I'll never know. The land was no reassurance for it reeled and bucked under my feet. We'd tidied and dried out the cabin as best we could. I think we needed a break from *Anassa*, as she maybe did from us. She'd had no qualms. She rode the anchor as deuce and neat as a little filly, perky for the next day's adventure.

We went ashore to get diesel and food. My childlike condition, once I stepped on dry land and tried to walk was further manifested when we had supper in the café, wet outer gear shed in a puddle at the door. All I wanted was chips and peas in this room that rose and fell, rose and fell. Not beans. Peas for some strange reason. They were absolutely delicious. I had seconds and thirds of peas alone. The Captain had a steak with all the trimmings and banoffie pie and cheese and coffee. I noticed he had taken off the red, black-spotted bandana.

I do not remember going back sodden in the sodden dinghy. I was numb to all discomfort. The damp bunk was as a linen-sheeted four-poster bed with goose down pillows. Davy Jones was my hot water bottle. I'd had the hot toddy several times.

I slept for ten hours and woke to thirteen bruises and a reluctance to get up. The rain it raineth still, pockmarking a soft desultory swell. Wraiths of mist on either headland lifted and parted like stage curtains announcing the next act of the play in which this character did not want to perform.

We took the diesel train from damp Arisaig to sunny Fort William just in time to rush to Safeway for hummus, olives, taramasalata, herb oatcakes, strawberries, cream, vinho verde and more, and get on the *Jacobite* steam train fired up to head back in the direction we'd just come. The sun came with us westwards the whole way. It was pure luxury sitting in the warmth of the old-fashioned carriage, legs stretched out, stringed luggage hammocks swaying above, the rucksacks atop filled with fresh treats for *Anassa*'s lockers. The high ones.

Crossing the railway bridge at the bottom of Neptune's Staircase at down-locking time was a weird kind of déjà vue in reverse. There they all were, the large and the small – yachts, cruisers, workboats – waiting for the train to pass and the bridge to be lifted for their passage along the final stretch of canal before the open sea. It seemed a lifetime ago that we had been doing just that. It had been a hot sunny day, too. Had Fort William, of all places, kept the summer to herself?

The Captain and I sat opposite; ate, drank, watched the unthreatening, predictable, benign gold mountains and dark green woods rattle past, picture postcard blue sky behind. We didn't talk. The interval of leisure too precious to waste with words. No decisions to be made; neither of us at the helm. We were being taken on an outing, somebody else leading the way. Such sweet combined surrender.

The acrid smell of coal smoke sifted through the carriages reminding me of the daily journey to school by train. Hanging out the window as the train puffed round the elegant arc of the Glenfinnan viaduct the memory was complete when I got the statutory cinder in my eye. At Glenfinnan station the train stopped. Breathing heavily, like a hard-worked animal grateful for rest, it gathered strength for the onward journey to Arisaig and Mallaig beyond.

A piper and a railway museum entertained passengers until the train got its breath back. The track was high above a twisting river making for the sea. Then Loch Ailort, and Loch nam Uamh, where the Bonnie Prince's disaster started and finished, sparkling Mediterranean blue. Looking down on Arisaig harbour we could make out the tiny dot of *Anassa* in amongst a forest of masts. So relaxed had we been by our day we had not realised this sentimental train journey was geared towards tourists and only stopped at Glenfinnan and Mallaig before returning to Fort William. Actually being able to point out *Anassa* from the carriage window as the train tooted unfettered downhill and recount a sob story about 'vital supplies' (true) for the boat, only obtainable from Fort William etc., persuaded the guard to contact the engine driver and an unscheduled stop was permitted at Arisaig, for which we were very grateful.

A gentle sun-lounging late afternoon and evening on deck reintroduced us to *Anassa*, dry as a bone. By the quirk of a slack tide eddy she persisted in facing out to sea, dwarfed by the large yachts all around which naturally faced inland on their moorings and anchors. It was as if she was saying, 'OK, you've had your fun. Now get me out of this dormitory.' Tomorrow, *Anassa*. Tomorrow.

The Rock

We renavigate Murdo Grant's admirable perches. Though no sun comes through the land mist yet, we know it will. We brought it back from Fort William, after all. A tall white-sailed yacht glides past to starboard.

There is not a drop of wind and her pale grey-blue hull is suspended over an identical colour and tone of water, Sargasso-thick with silvered seaweed. A ghost ship. The silence pleased me. No Force 7 today. A simple uneventful passage to Loch Nevis lay ahead. If the sun comes out, I might even get that elusive sunbathe on deck, the Mediterranean blue sparkling past, white seagulls planing overhead, the sparkling wine. With tentative confirmation the sun wove through the limpid morning.

The Captain is exploring other ideas. The break from *Anassa* has fired him up even more about his life's ambition to live on a boat. 'She'll be bigger than *Anassa*, of course. A converted MFV, 60 feet or thereabouts, twin Gardiner engines. There would be a huge, fully equipped galley with a Rayburn stove. And a covered verandah up over the stern with steamer chairs and wicker tables for the gin and tonics. Hot showers; and heads that I can stand up and turn around in.' If *Anassa* has a heart she must be mortally wounded.

We are long past the last perch. No more need for caution. The jib is up and toys with what little wind there is. Soon we are out, turning north, the engine at full throttle. For once the Captain is not peeved by the lack of wind, too involved in plans for his dream boat.

Down in *Anassa*'s tiny galley I smile as I prepare new fresh vegetables for soup. The kettle has just come off the boil for coffee. I've transferred it to the broad step up into the cockpit, to place the soup pot on the vacated ring. The other ring simmers greasy tea towels.

In the split second of impact I am flung backwards, my upper spine and back of my head whacked on the mast support as I fall, hot kettle water drenching my trousers. I know the engine has blown up, but can't get to my feet before the ship surely does. I am winded, that frightening paralysis, that tightens chest and throat to panic point. I hear the engine reversing furiously, the Captain's hand is pulling me out of the cabin as I gasp and choke, 'What's happened?'

We are aground. *Anassa*'s engine labours in reverse. The rocks are wavering vivid and clear less than four feet below water level. Cream and white and pink with constellations of barnacles clinging to their peaked contours. I see every single crustacean of the tens of thousands in the minutest detail. I notice there is no seaweed evilly, darkly weaving around them. The barnacles are as bright little jewels, sunlight caught with flickering refraction.

I've registered that *Anassa* is on an even keel. That is more important to me than anything and gives me confidence, which is further bolstered after I've limped down into the cabin and find no evidence of water gushing in. The Captain wrestles with sharp bursts of reverse. With a loud scrunching of pulverised barnacles against the lead of the keel, she wriggles backwards, freed. We are miles off shore. No such rock exists on the chart. I sense the Captain's shock. I saw the whites of his eyes. He is silent. There is no easy banter this time. I am amazed at my calmness. I realise I have finally accepted it all. All of it – the bridge at Inverness, the sandbank at Kessock, the 'slack' of Loch Etive, the storm, the rock off Morar. They are all par for the course in a yacht at sea. Why did nobody tell me?

Chopped vegetables and soup stock slither all over my bunk. The greasy tea towels, unperturbed, still simmer away. I am further amazed at my new fearless capacity to stay below and tidy up. Recriminations, reconstructions are the last thing the Captain is in the mood for. My back and head are thudding pain. These will be big bruises. I think of all the engineers deep in the bowels of wartime ships and now understand their stoicism. Better to keep down below and not know a thing of what is going on up above. Just get on with the job in hand.

Fuel-starved engines, sandbanks, tidal tyrannies, chart datum rocks and such other unknowns ahead no longer frighten me. Till now the promise of returning to Loch Etive has, privately, lain covert and trembling like a rabid cur, in my thoughts, waiting to leap like my other self-created monsters and pull me down to the bottomless pit that is their breeding ground. No more. The initiation is over.

I fill the kettle and prepare to make coffee again. The splash of sunlight that illuminated the barnacles has gone. A great bank of sea mist is coming ghosting over from the Small Isles. We are really far out now and, just before visibility falls to 50 feet we see two yachts heading south, close into land on the very line we had initially embarked on.

The Captain is speechless. I try to cheer him with coffee and Brazil nut chocolate and read out contrived reassurance from Rachel Carson's *The Sea Around Us*:

> In modern times we have never seen the birth of an island as large as
> Ascension. But now and then there is a report of a small island
> appearing where none was before. Perhaps a month, a year, five years
> later, the island has disappeared into the sea again. These are the little
> stillborn islands doomed to only a brief emergence above the sea.

He would not wear it. 'I've been on Ascension Island. "New" islands are volcanic. There is no volcanic activity in this part of the world. I disobeyed my own golden rule. I was not well enough out to sea to make passage.' This is said with such finality, despite my muttering about the Caledonian Faultline and Ascension Island being in the Atlantic, albeit the South. In my new frame of mind I knew that rock was still rising and I had been party to a miracle that should be celebrated and broadcast wide. I wondered if the two yachts had noticed it. They would get the praise and acclaim if they had, damn it.

Morose with the mist, now compounded by torrential rain, we slowly steam north-east, the Little Bastard in command. Everything is steaming. Drips come down on my head in the cabin as I go on reading. 'About 1830 such an island suddenly appeared in the Mediterranean between Sicily and the coast of Africa, rising from 100 fathom depths …'

Cheery shouts come from on deck. The *Aurora* from Orkney, our old companion from the Canal, is hoving to. We bemoan the weather, but the fishing has proved good for them. The black dog pokes her nose out of the wheelhouse, withdrawing back into the dry with a sigh. It is a good interlude. A bit like a valuable conversation in a foggy bus station late at night before first one and then the other traveller go their separate ways. I can tell the Captain's mood is easing with all the man talk. And as *Aurora* swirls off with an engine power that would spear through Etive narrows whatever the state of the tide, the sea mist lifts as light as gossamer, and the sun, quite unapologetic, for it is always there shining, gets on with its journey. Great blue bands of sky lift from the south, little shreds of white cloud still low down on the hills of Knoydart, Arisaig and Moidart – the Rough Bounds, so called for their rugged nature.

We are heading past Morar and Mallaig for Loch Nevis, the northerly and most remote Bound of the district, our spirits lifting with the clearing skies. Not a drop of tell-tale water, bilge or other, seeps into the cabin. 'What that keel was built for, y'know!' The Captain is back on form.

Loch Nevis

Roadless on either side, Loch Nevis is only inhabited at the head of the loch by those who caretake Camusrory Estate and the landowner when in residence. Their access is by sea, the route we are navigating. Mallaig, the nearest rail and road head, is about twenty miles distant – weather permitting. The roofless croft of Stoul passes to starboard, witness, as are like ruins along the lochside, to a not-so-distant living past. At Tarbet and the narrows of Kylesknoydart and Kylesmorar with track access, cottages have been done up with serious Southern money, the cost of importing as expensive, if not more so, than the materials. Silently they watch us go by with shuttered eyes. A kind of confused anger wells up inside. It is good that the stones are saved from final collapse and returned to the land whence they came, but there is a foreign feel despite traditional immaculate reconstruction; an alienness compounded by 'Private' signs easily legible as *Anassa* slips close by through the narrows. Here, truly at the back of beyond, the only potential marauders are deer and hillwalkers. Or maybe pirates.

Inner Loch Nevis is like glass. The mountains on either side are white-streaked with rushing burns and waterfalls; the white, clinging land clouds evaporated in the warm, healing afternoon sun. After the storm, the calm.

'Wouldst thou' – so the helmsman answered, –
'Learn the secret of the sea?
Only those who brave its dangers
Comprehend its mystery!

[*The Secret of the Sea* Longfellow]

Dinner
is Served...

This will be our most isolated anchorage so far. I have long looked forward to it. Supper looks good too. Three mackerel lie gutted and glistening in the bucket. The three of them, the three of us, the mountains, the sea and not a soul else for evening repast.

What is this need of mine for yet further isolation in a landscape which is intrinsically isolated anyway? In the past, this need became a passion that led to an obsession to own plots of land and houses positioned in the most splendid isolation. Ownership clinching not just earthly territory, but the view as far as the eye could see without tarnishing evidence of another human being. Always, in time, extensions were added on to possess yet another angle of the view when familiarity diluted its essence. Windows framed landscapes and seascapes as in an art gallery, priceless, Not for Sale. What envy all around! These things have been, many times. The site, no matter how unique, always became a trap.

Anassa is showing me another way of possessing, transitory though it may be yet with many more riches. The wilderness places will always be there. Waiting. Quite unmoved by the cycle of desertion, reclamation, desertion. The owners of the pristine cottages at the Kyles are, undoubtedly, as needful as me to tap into this life balm that gives respite from the helter-skelter, hugger-mugger of most of contemporary living.

Thanks to *Anassa* my 'possession' of the wilderness places is a moveable feast with no encumbrances of community charge, title deed or padlock. I was learning that the title deeds of the soul are more rewarding than those of the land. Maybe I need never own property again. Imagine my – and the Captain's – distress at another yacht already anchored at the head of the loch, walkers with backpacks on the Knoydart side, whelk gatherers on the shore! As though mocking, three tiny figures look down on us from the 3,410-feet peak of Sgurr na Ciche. Another boat comes up the loch looking for anchorage. I hold my title deeds close to my chest all night.

It worked. Next day everyone is gone. We move *Anassa* to the prime anchorage at the head of the loch.

Windless, in the bowl of the crater of mountains, a light tapestry of sounds weaves in and around *Anassa*. The hillside burns are slowing, updraughts of air current intermittently cut out their down-rush and the silence is filled with the faint early rut roar of a high stag. A hairy oatmeal seal sleeps perpendicular nearby, its head limpidly rising and falling, its snout pointing to heaven. The bulk of its body is tapering thin and shadowy into the clear water which the morning sun bathes right through to sand, two fathoms below. The sand stretches from shore to shore and for a mile down the loch with little deepening. Yes, I will swim today.

The seal is quite oblivious to the strident ululation of a pair of oystercatchers who are inland in a perfect semi-circle, the hills echoing their temporary distress before the silence descends again only interrupted by those air currents that rise to stroke the high peaks with deceptive swoons. In the slack of a very high tide, the dinghy is looped round, nudging *Anassa*. It squeaks like a nest of baby mice. A porpoise undulates lazily across our bow at this so very inland spot. Have shoals of refugee fish come flowing through the narrows all those miles back only to be caught by its smooth intelligence? A flock of herons, eight or more, flap leisurely across the loch and appear to land on an inhospitable hillside. But it is a little scruffy wood perched precariously as they. Their home, their heronry. A final get-together of this year's siblings before the lonely vigils of adulthood by loch and river edge.

The Captain is in the galley. The spit and crackle of a Greasy Joe stitch into the tapestry. What price the title deeds to all this?

The dramatically high spring tide meant a long dinghy row to shore. A day in the hills lay ahead treading old ground. Like Penmeanach, there is a Mountain Bothy Association base at Sourlies just inland from the loch that had seen many a family gathering twenty-odd years previously. The walk in was an arduous six to eight miles from the end of the Loch Arkaig road, but the final climb to the 1,000 foot pass before zigzagging down to tiny Sourlies below was worth it.

Little had changed. The soot-blackened chimney breast and pots, the empty malt whisky bottle holding the stub of a candle, the bothy books, mice-nibbled and damp-warped, the notice to replace all firewood. Bothy books are always an interesting mix of erudition, puerility, and overblown prose and poetry. The 1992 edition had an

· Loch Nevis ·

historic welcome and introduction by the then new landowners of the Camusrory Estate. A kind of apologia for being landowners threads through the text which describes Camusrory as a 'low level sporting estate' comprising deerstalking, fishing and recreational lets 'conducted with a degree of activity which keeps the invasive element to a minimum.' The meat of the message comes towards the end, advising that there are no rescue services available but help as much as possible will be given even though EU rulings on public liability are now an issue. 'You may be asked to sign a disclaimer form if we were to apply medication or provide transport in any form. Yes, I know it sounds stupid but we are amateurs in this case and we didn't start all this ... Please enjoy your visit but tread softly and carefully.'

The present owners have declined to add any of their own addendums but are also reputed to believe in the softly, softly approach to hillwalkers.

The Captain is confused. 'I think I'd rather have the old days of the aristocratic Colonel Blimps roaring through snuff-stained whiskers telling people to "Bugger off or I'll shoot!" Nine times out of ten, if you stood your ground, they'd have you in for a drink. Not this psuedo apologetic EU rulings lot.'

On both sides of the fence the gelding of initiative is proceeding with caution.

The track up to the pass is the remnant of the drove road that walked cattle and sheep from Knoydart and North Morar through Glen Dessary last century and the century before, to meet up with herds from Skye en route for the markets of Falkirk and Stirling. Towards the summit the incline is eased with stone-buttressed and paved zigzags as perfect as the day they were masoned and fashioned into place. To walk such tracks brings to mind the hundreds of people, in trade or war or social communication, that trod before us. I fancy their spirits lingering but some, like a baton in a relay race, eager to be grasped and carried forward.

It was exhilarating to be so high. We climbed on higher into a hanging valley where at 1,000 foot, mountains and scree all around, fertile grassland showed evidence of summer shielings, transhumance. The only stock to be seen now was a resting hind and calf but fifty yards away, quite unperturbed by our trespass. We lost all sense of time. Part of me did not want to go back to *Anassa*.

'Let's go higher!' I was in my true element where no dragons lay in wait, where each step I took was mine and mine alone; the decision to take this route or that up the hillside my own unfettered responsibility. I felt a fluidity in my body like that of a mountain goat. Up I went, the sky the limit.

'Well! Well!' drawled the Captain as we took breath on an outcrop below the top of Sgurr na Ciche. He was looking down through the binoculars at the loch glittering small below. '*Anassa*'s aground!'

'*What*?'

She was, starboard gunwale to the sand, high and dry. The tide was away with the fish and the porpoise, the seal and the herons half way to the narrows. I could not understand the Captain's lack of reaction. With adrenalin in reverse I started to run downhill towards the disaster. Guilt tripping up my stumbling panic. This was worse than leaving a sleeping child in a pram outside a supermarket or, even worse, in an empty house with faulty electrical wiring. Will *Anassa* ever forgive us? We had betrayed her for the hills. Unforgivable.

'Calm down! Calm down! It is called careening,' wheezed the Captain when he caught up with me. 'Quite in order. A perfect place; all that gently shelving sand. And a good opportunity to inspect the hull and keel after our little altercation with The Rock.'

The tide was coming in, unrepentant. We ankle-waded out to her sad, listed hulk, beached like a whale, so inelegant. 'She is *humiliated*,' I told the Captain; but he was already engrossed in satisfactorily checking the keel, poking every plank and seam and then burnishing the prop blades with Brillo Pads. For her own good yet this seemed like a further intimate abuse of her awkward position. A sort of naval smear test.

The cabin was like a Marie Celeste space capsule where gravity had gone beserk. The gimballed oil lamps and cooker were frozen at 45 degrees. Anything hanging was similarly angled, the pencil on its string by the chart table, the hurricane lamp from the ceiling, the red and black spotted neckerchief and a shirt from the mast support hooks. Books, rugs, bedding were lumped on the cabin floor which was really a sloping left-hand wall; the starboard bulwark a curved floor. Lewis Carroll must have experienced a careening.

There was no point in trying to realign the out-of-order phenomena. Nature caused it and would right it. With potholing contortion I retrieved the bottle of Pernod rolled in-between pages 44 and 45 of *Cruiser Management*. As ever the herbs were unperturbed at gravity's joke, wedged behind the doghouse door. The cooker being on the 'down' side had the half-full kettle slithered but gently resting on the starboard cooker rail.

The whole keeling-over process must have taken about four slow hours of minute by gentle minute inclination, the keel settling into the suckling sand. Hardly perceptible, the inch by inch outflow of the tide took away *Anassa's* element and lowered her esteem to the dried-out seabed. Did the porpoise and the seal weave and wonder by her metamorphosis; did the herons cock an interested eye? I almost wish I had seen it happen. From the shore. I was certainly most glad I had not forgone the mountain walk. Heavens, I could have been alone in the cabin asleep, the captain a'chasing the deer …

We had to leave her when the tide reached our thighs. The Captain had realigned the anchor chain. We both knew she would rather handle her resurrection like a wet phoenix on her own. Wading back to shore and the far off dinghy we registered the sun was well over the yardarm. Burn water milked the Pernod to perfection.

Unplanned events bring bonuses. The upper shore was littered with small rocks heavily encrusted with the biggest of mussels all of three inches long. Nick Nairn eat your heart out for mussel steaks with garlic and chive butter. We also had time to muse on the voyage so far and where we were going next. We were way behind the schedule envisaged those winter months ago. To begin with we had tried, but conspiracies, primarily of those ever-dictating tides, had shifted rigid prescribed attainment to the freedom of an unconditional continuum, elastic in its expectations. Maybe we had gone nautically native.

'We're actually a week behind,' the Captain worked out. 'We should be heading for Loch Leven on the return route by now.' We had saved Loch Leven for

· The 'Careening' · Loch Nevis ·

the last fjord. Not only did the Glencoe and Ballachulish mountains edge its waters, an ancient wooded burial island with stones from Celtic to Victorian times had always attracted my attention the many times I had driven past on the A82. It is called Eilean Munde or the Isle of the Dead. I wanted to spend a night on it.

And with that focus in mind, for the Voyage of *Anassa* could not go on for ever, we up-anchored after re-establishing order in the cabin and headed towards the end of the day for Tarbet, a tiny inlet back down the loch.

From the west, the slanting sun picked out acres of lazybed ridges on the hillside behind Stoul, now to port. Un-lazybed ridges. What time and labour dragging seaweed there. To have seen them in production. Never recorded, only to be imagined.

The echo sounder just won't go below 10 to 15 fathoms as we edge nearer and nearer the steep shelving shingle shore of Tarbet Bay. The evening is pin-drop quiet and darkening. I whisper out the soundings above the just-ticking-over engine, mindful of, incongruously, a brightly lit church whose parish seems to consist of but one cottage, which also sheds golden light on the shore but not on an anchorage. Both are but a stone's throw from the water's edge. The inlet is so narrow we turn apprehensively for another attempt. The pilot book says 'good anchorage for small vessels with local knowledge'. Local knowledge rows over from the one other anchored boat in the dimming gold-edged light. Squat and spread the width of his dinghy, a holey brown jumper coating, like moss, the rotundity of his upper torso, old green wellies, knitted bunnet with a salt-caked and sundried pompom atop; this did not look like a yachtie. Neither was his boat of that description. It was an old converted lifeboat sleekly silhouetted against the gold and silver shredding sky. 'Yer fine, yer fine! Drop anchor now. I'll hear your craic in the morning. I saw your careening this afternoon.' And off he paddles. Faint strains of Jimmy Shand Scottish Country Music come from the bowels of his life-saving boat. A seal called Oatmeal blends in with watery wheezes, and once *Anassa*'s engine is cut, the slow muffled thud-a-thud of a generator on the land gives the base beat to a solo blackbird in the wood behind the cottage. Its last song of the day as pure as the velvet-dark silence patiently waiting to bed us all down. But it isn't last light yet; a long-tailed harrier screeches defiantly above the wood. Not bedtime, quite.

I wonder who lives in the cottage in this lonely spot. The luminosity of its walls indicates recent whitewash. Another holiday cottage? The profligate church still glows warm light from its arched latticed windows, reflected traceries of liquid gold criss-crossing over the dark water to *Anassa*. Was it an all-night wake, a coffin on trestles by the altar? No one had come in or out of the building or the cottage since we had anchored. As though to end further conjecture the lights of both went suddenly out and the generator died with a cough. The coffin to be shrouded in peace.

It was midnight before the dinosauric mussels from the head of Loch Nevis let the boiling water seep into their thick clamped maws. An hour's wait for the mussel 'steaks'. Not very Nick Nairn, actually, but we were ravenous.

Old Donald's cockerel woke me at 6 am. The crowing was incongruous so near to *Anassa*. But daylight showed how intimate was Tarbet Bay to the land. The cottage *was* immaculately whitewashed; windows, doors and slating recently traditionally replaced but it was no holiday cottage. Chanticleer strutted his womenfolk into feather-flattening submission one after the other. The day was started. Donald stood outside his smart crofthouse surveying his naval neighbours. He and *Lifeboat* are old buddies. But who were we?

His house is the last to be inhabited by a local the length of Loch Nevis's southern shores. In his nineties, Donald, now widowed, is stooped, but the tall refined man in him, belonging to generations of crofter fisherfolk who lived and worked all their lives in this wilderness area, is still manifest. The church was where the community worshipped, some walking many miles in all weathers. It is now a walkers' hostel, no coffin inside, carefully converted in keeping with its Catholic history; pews, refectory table and heavy ornate candlesticks are a set piece for the mediaeval theatre of Boccacchio's *Decameron*. The Madonna blue of the altar stowed up in the gallery looks down on wooden handmade bunks. Someone with

Tarbet

money, taste and flair has created this little-used sanctuary. The light is always left on should a late walker arrive.

Not all that long ago Donald and Jessie ran the loneliest post office in Britain from the crofthouse. In the hey-day of Tom McLean's Adventure Centre in the 1970s and 1980s at Ardintigh, roadless over the hill southwards, the MacDonalds were not only the postal but hospitable link with the outside world.

Further afield, or rather, asea, Inverie in Knoydart was, and is, the nearer official hostelry than Mallaig and still the one preferred by Donald. He was getting ready to go over in the Estate boat, best tweed jacket over shirt and tie, to a birthday party Welcome Home for the hostel warden, who is returning from the South via Mallaig that afternoon. Inverie is more geographically remote, yet has a strong resident community.

Asking, the way one does of old people, what are the biggest changes, Donald answered simply, 'The speed of things.' Then added, 'And lots more water from the spoot.' The outside water pipe agreed, sparkling out a steady flow from a hillside tank hidden high in the foliage. 'And the water inside the house is fine too, from the taps!'

Donald's landlord is Cameron MacIntosh, theatre producer, who has an historical and personal attitude to his responsibility. As a boy he used to stay with his uncle who, retired from Far East tea planting, had set up a carpentry shop in Mallaig and built a Martha's Vineyard type log cabin overlooking Tarbet Bay. When the surrounding Estate came up for sale there was no question in adult Cameron MacIntosh's mind. Locally, the ownership of the land is comfortably accepted. *Lifeboat* endorsed this when we had the promised bit of 'craic'. 'The only one I've met that I have no gripe with. A good chiel at heart.'

The 'theatre' of the hostel is thanks to the 'good chiel'. Not so are things opposite in Knoydart where there are no indigenous people left. In the past twelve years there have been three owners of the estate, shadowy business figures who flit in in helicopters, part asset strip, then sell the reduced acreage to another of their kind. Approximately seventy people live there and more would if there was security. The Knoydart Community Association have speared the initiative to create The Knoydart Foundation. The long journey ahead, like that of Eigg, will hopefully become yet another example of achieved viable stability for modern-day communities in remote areas. Things *are* changing, but slowly. It is not so easy for old-style irresponsible and arrogant landowners to dictate as once they did. As recently as 1948, Knoydart men returning from the war to impoverished crofts laid claim to unused arable land and were ruthlessly defeated.

As we sailed over to Inverie – 'Of course, you'll come to the birthday party!' Donald had stated, matter of factly – the Captain sang loudly and lustily:

> It was down by the farm of Scottas
> Lord Brockett walked one day
> Where he saw a sight that troubled him
> Far more than he could say.
> For the *Seven Men of Knoydart*
> Were doing what they planned;
> They had staked their claims,
> They were digging drains
> On Brockett's Private Land.

A more universal memorial to that time of failure is inscribed on the cairn in Inverie village: 'History will judge harshly the oppressive laws that have led to the virtual extinction of a unique culture from this beautiful place.' Not that long ago many parts of the Highlands and Islands of Scotland were treated like Third World Countries, a phrase unknown then and I use with no circumspection now.

Talking in the pub, balloons and streamers, paper hats (Donald's was pink) celebrating Frank's seventieth, was no time or place to dig deep into politics, but I remember someone saying, 'The Seven Men of Knoydart weren't the right men for the job.' And saying no more. I suppose in a cryptic way he was underlining what I was beginning to see more clearly. The times are a-changing; old socialist principles are fading. Individualism respected yet strongly bonded within communities can be constructive, not disseminating. There are certainly many individuals in Knoydart with a very common purpose. I wish them luck.

I looked at Donald and saw an old man who is not locked into the past, a long past which could have so easily carried cultural alienness and bitterness forward into his final years. To what purpose? He was enjoying the present; maybe he had all his life. With no side, no politics. Doors open then.

The capitalist rapist owners of Knoydart missed a good opportunity that day. After the third rendering in the pub of 'The Wild Rover' it was time to get a breath of fresh air. Bizarrely, a rusted tub of a boat, high sided with one open-side hatch revealing jam-packed gesticulating humans inside, was tying up at the pier. They were klondykers from a Russian fish factory ship moored halfway to Mallaig. There is no Harbour Master or Customs Officer in Inverie. Black market cigarettes are bartered for legitimate booze. And whatever else. Venison? Two very mini-skirted women also climb out of the boat. Not Mallaig 'ladies of the pier heid' but Russian too. Trapped with their men in a stinking floating factory that is home. Fish followers. Nobody hangs about long. Deals are swiftly concluded and the men and the two women return in the rust-red box of a tender to Mother Russia. I go to the shop. It has been supply day for it too. With a recidivism I cannot attempt to excuse, I buy CHICKEN BURGERS and FISH FINGERS from the freezer cabinet! What is happening?

En fête, I gather replacement wildflowers for the jam-jar. The Captain and I regroup to *Anassa* and a pre-arranged rendezvous with *Lifeboat*. We have little diesel and the tide demands early departure on the morrow if we want to move on. Many plastic containers are marshalled in lines and strapped to *Lifeboat*'s deck. *Lifeboat* was *Faireaq* all those years ago and still lives the life of the Captain's ambition, spending the summers cruising the West Coast, just going home every so often 'to cut the grass'. The highlight of the Skipper's solitary circumnavigations is when a yacht is in distress. He listens by the hour to Channel 16 on the VHF, which is the coastguard channel. The wheelhouse is banked with the latest navigational aides. The Little Bastard is but a digital wristwatch in comparison. Visual steering must be so limited given the banks of bleeping screens. Yet all is covered in a layer of tired dust. As though the gizmos were reluctantly collected. Because *Lifeboat* still wants to be a lifeboat? The old guidelines still obtain, however. 'When the barometer falls below 960 millibars, time to stay put.' The Captain is in seventh heaven. As he eyestrokes the massive diesels, I trawl over *Lifeboat*'s library in the sealed-off fore cabin where rescued sailors were lowered in from the foredeck to be incarcerated till harbour was reached. The *Life and Times of Adolf Hitler* sat side by side with Clyde Cruising Club manuals.

Lifeboat wouldn't take a penny for the diesel, even though we declined his invite to chum him northwards next day. Our time was running out and southwards it had to be for us.

Back on *Anassa* the hubbub from the pub is convoyed over the darkling water by a light breeze with bursts of Shirley Bassey singing 'Hey! Big Spender'. 'The Wild Rover' accordionist has given up. A dinghy goes splashing past, rowed by the silhouette of a young woman who still hums his tune.

Long before Donald's cockerel announced the dawn in far off Tarbet, *Anassa* was under way. Inverie was dark and deeply asleep, first intimations of light angled over the southern hills of North Morar, eerily illuminating flat coastal swathes of

· *Inverie* ·

long-deserted grazings. Since the burnishing of *Anassa*'s prop the Captain is convinced we go faster and plans a *coup de marée*. 'With six hours tide flowing south and adding to that a couple of hours slack, we'll get to the Sound of Mull in time for the turn and be carried right up to Strontian at the head of Loch Sunart!' Looking at my preferred OS map it looked like a very long way and day ahead. I had enjoyed the social interaction of Inverie. I prepared myself for the reduction of dualism. Vowing not to duel. I busied myself with a Greasy Fish Finger Joe. It was 5am and the ghost-like Madonna of Knoydart looked down on our oleaginous passing with benefaction.

The day promised good but it was cold up on deck. The dawning was not to be missed, however. We pass, *Anassa* so tiny, the towering cathedral of the klondyker;

Inverie Bay
5 Fathoms
(57° 25'N 5° 44'W)
fm '98

lights sparkle and twinkle, all-night clanking machinery processes fish into cans. But I know it is venison burgers for the workers' breakfast this morning.

Ahead, low-fluffed clouds stitched to the tops of Rum and Eigg are lit white-gold. Behind, the clouds are banked, dark, ghostly-grey over the black outline of Knoydart's Ladhar Beinn. Coming out into the Sound of Sleat there is a slight choppy swell. On with the wristbands. Second by second the world is lightening. Mallaig, unseen on the sea-misted northward passage, is bright and white, dotted with houses. At the harbour the *Pioneer*'s cheery red funnel marks the point of departure for Armadale on Skye. A skelf of a moon gives in to the ever-circular sun's arising.

Not quite as dangerous as at the wheel of a car (we are miles out from The Rock of Arisaig), I actually fall asleep at the helm and give in to the luxury of a kip in my bunk. Like a baby in a pram I let the Captain and the tide push me wherever they want. I'll wake at feeding time.

The bleak line of the island is an infinite raft of threads on the horizon. Parallel and above, a black lanuginous cloud slowly smothers the sun. A bitter wind whistles up pewter waves. Do I dream up a storm to bind me with endless entangled threads?

I see the church tower on the hill, a marker so familiar, in line with the green conical buoy. I slip *Anassa* in past the empty pier and on to a mooring opposite the village. So unfamiliar; to be here but not quite, for the water is still in between. No one knows I am here. Gently bobbing up and down, I can view the island anonymously. A world I know so intimately, but the islanders know nothing of this new limbo world of mine. They see only another yachite arrived in the bay.

The hotelier checks his wine cellar. The fishermen shell the prawns quickly, ask their wives how many clams are left in the freezer and are glad there were lobsters in the creels this morning. The potter curses an untimely firing in the pier shed but tests the hire bike brakes in practical anticipation. The craft shop will stay open a bit later, most likely.

A tractor and trailer stops and starts along the street. It is Saturday, rubbish collection day. Children's voices punctuate the short spaces between the two shops, the post office and the playpark. In the schoolhouse up the brae the teacher is planning a holiday. The old ferryman walks slowly to the first shop, then the other, then the post office for the second time today. He doesn't really need that other packet of biscuits or the second class stamp but he never knows what else he might glean beside the counters before the day is done.

Intermittently, vehicles of varying age and condition are driven into 'town' from outlying areas. I know by the variegated tones of rust and the bass fractured tones of exhausts of some of them that the itinerant policeman is not visiting the island.

Do they know I have come to visit? It doesn't matter. The cloud is lifted and so am I. Above the raft of threads.

Cipherlike I weave in and out of the old haunts. The islanders can't see me; they are too preoccupied. I leave the village and follow the coastline gliding through the air a few feet above the edge of the sea. I look downwards as though I am a swimmer in another element. The sunlight reaches through the water to gloss the pebbles, marble the sand and shred the fronds of brilliant green seaweed. At the water's edge it warms the pink necklaces of tideline cowries that lead to the house on the wild headland.

It is as I left it, stubborn and alone, cold empty floors gathering dust, curtainless windows staring blankly over the dancing sea and the sparkling dunes; the wood lining of the kitchen bereft of its idiosyncratic paraphernalia. High old-fashioned coathooks and the low ones for the children point at me, bare and accusing, through the porch window. There is a dead starling on the window-sill of the sitting-room. The grapes, for the first time ever, have matured in the conservatory.

But I don't have the key to the house any more. The house awaits new keys and eddies of air to sweep away the dust and detritus, to sweeten the grapes.

I'm down on the ground now and wade through the forest of weeds in the garden. Such produce was cultivated here. I did not often have to go to the village – to collect the mail, latterly, that was all.

And then I remember with old familiar panic. The post office shuts early on Saturdays! I'm running and running along the beach scattering the cowries, the sand dragging me down. Then I'm on the moor stumbling in and out of sucking bogs and ditches. The smothering black wool cloud is descending, the trapped wind pushes me backwards. I *must* get there in time.

In the village people are standing about battered by the storm, water streaming down their faces, saying it was time the old ways were changing. The post office is just closing. My mud and sandflecked toe is in the door. 'But there's nothing for you here,' says the postmistress with concern. 'Your mail has all been forwarded to the mainland, as you requested.'

Anassa has broken from her mooring and is drifting out to sea. I am screaming at one of the fishermen to take me out to her …

'Feeding time,' said the Captain.

The chicken burgers were foul and went over the side. A single gannet floating by with buttery cream neck feathers was surprised and disdainful. Not so a herring gull whose tastebuds are junkified by human food remains in dumps and city centres. I still cannot quite believe I am safely aboard *Anassa*.

It was nearly midday but the Captain declined my offer of relief from the helm. He was obviously enjoying the challenge of harnessing the tide and wind. Both sails were up. We were doing 7.4 knots, the Little Bastard said. I sat at the bow, feet dangling over each side. The motion was like that of a half-tamed bronco, bucking out of habit just for the sheer enjoyment. There were lots of yachts out and about, some crossing our bows with cavalier flourish but *Anassa* was not to be deflected from her determined course. Underneath the surface waves the body of the sea rose and fell in immense rolls. Terns angrily chided a raft of rollercoasting guillemots. The mainland stretch from Mallaig to Ardnamurchan was a grey-blue ribbon of crumpled and tweaked hills. The labial folds of the headlands on either side of the entrance to Loch Moidart reminded me of the hidden treasures within. And stolen property.

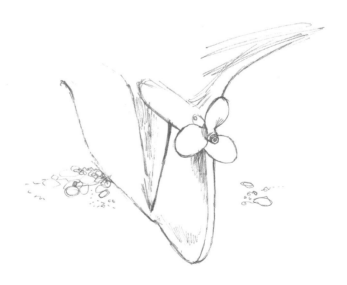

Loch Sunart

Entering the Sound of Mull the familiar turbulence of tidal change confirmed we were on target. For all the years I have travelled up and down the Sound of Mull to the island I have never noticed the entrance to Loch Sunart. Another fjord entrance deceptively hidden. The little islands of Oronsay and Risga with Carna behind appear as a low land link between Ardnamurchan and Morven. Loch Sunart is nineteen miles in length and will be our longest inlet so far, comparable with Loch Etive to come.

Porpoises curve in with us. Out go the mackerel traces. Maybe there will be real fish for supper. The lump of Carna seals off the sea. Red sandstone-turreted Glenborrodale Castle peeps over treed rocks to port. Like so many mansions it faces east. Victorians started their Highland day bathed in the rays of the rising sun, as did their dead relatives and retainers in nearby grave-yards. A daily resurrection. One physical, the other spiritual. To build a house facing the dying day too dangerously decadent? I would do that if I could.

The loch is mirror calm and houses along its wooded sides are reflected in the still water. Several log cabins and half-wooded chalets give a distinct Nordic feel to the fjord. There is much forestry. So different from the wild bleakness of Loch Nevis. Was it only this morning we left? This is another country. Fish farm country. The surface of the water is becoming marled with skeins of aerated scum. Somewhere I have written that fish farming cages are 'the inevitable extension of man's age-old need to compartmentalise and control his environment. Fish cages are no more of an eyesore than fences.' These words belong to the land-based person I used to be, who looked down on a loch with its man-made water fields patchworked like those of the land. I have another perspective now. Anchorages mentioned in old pilot books are inaccessible, so prolific is the industry becoming in some sea lochs. Loch Sunart is no exception. And I could see the pollution at close quarters and actually touch it if I trailed my hand in the waters this calm sunny afternoon. There is much local feeling for and against fish farming. Most farms are owned by distant multi-nationals but give employment. The industry is worth £450 million a year to the Scottish economy. The wilderness lobby argue that controls are not tight enough; it is easier to get permission for a fish cage with no environmental or aesthetic criteria than get planning permission for a house extension of sympathetic vernacular design.

Rounding the elbow of the loch at Salen, the wind freshened. Ahead, according to Martin Lawrence's pilot book, there were 'some spectacular bits of rock dodging for those who have a taste for that sort of thing'. We have been aboard *Anassa* for nearly twelve hours and I am much more exhausted than the Captain. Like the

'Sound of Mull'

breeze, he is freshening. 'One of the rocks was discovered not to be in 25 metres as recorded but barely submerged. That was in 1979!' WHY does the Captain delight in telling me such facts when I DO NOT WANT TO KNOW? I remember my vow and go below and boil water for a big clothes wash that will keep me out the way.

We reach Strontian at the head of the loch uneventfully, *Anassa*'s rails festooned with flapping tea towels, T-shirts, knickers, the red and black spotted neckerchief, and anchor near *Hercules The Big Softy*, which has an orphaned look to it. No yachties here. 'In easterly winds there are violent squalls from the head of the loch.' The further freshening wind is from the east. After a quick foray but long walk into Strontian itself for water, long overdue family phonecalls, postcards, ice-cream and brandy, the Captain does not like *Anassa*'s tugging and bucking anchorage. 8.30 pm – we left Inverie at 4.30 am – we lift anchor and set off back down the loch, towards that circular sun, sloping down, preparing to bow out to an even skelfier moon. By post-prandial port and cigars at Laudale House the wind has provocatively dropped. A small rowboat, almost level with the peach, satin-chiffoned reflected water, has four silhouetted figures and two arc-ed rods aboard. We pass close, and they offer up their hip flasks in salutation if not transference. Streaks and layers of

puce-pinked clouds stratify into the ether behind them and then we become a silhouette to them. We are heading for an achorage east of Eilean Garbh on the opposite shore. Our longest day ends in a night of stars and silence. The Captain sleeps like a baby.

For me, the night was restless. I dreamt of Loch Etive, the dervish of its outfall as swirling as other worrying thoughts that focused on my homeless state that was soon to be ended. To just drift on was tempting; the new mainland life, not. All night *Anassa* seemed to be close to a fast-moving gurgling river. The tide race, I thought, but there was no surface movement in the night-black water. In daylight there it was again, a never-ending thrash and splash. It was farmed salmon, leaping and twisting in their prison cages near the opposite shore. With manic repetition they were jumping out of the water and slapping back down. Was this exuberant *joie de vivre* or a desperate activity to free them of the maddening irritation of sea lice? I didn't think I had any lice but there was a parallel of sorts. Was *Anassa* becoming a prison in which I had become institutionalised and now feared the ending of the sentence the nearer it came?

The day was burning hot but deceptively cool on board. The wind was 'on the nose' but slight. The engine motored us cheerily down Loch Sunart. I lay on deck oblivious to the beauty we were moving through, the journal and sketchbook closed and uninviting. I just wanted to be on holiday, an organised holiday with sun and sangria, the same bed location each night and no decisions to be made. A camp chair and a good book. I was reading *Iron Men, Wooden Women*, a collection of essays on Gender and Seafaring in the Atlantic World, 1700 to 1920. There were hundreds of women in a variety of guises who lived on board ship. Captain's wives could sometimes be years at sea, privileged yet deprived, often recording their experiences in journals as an aid to memory or because of habitual duty or the need for a private emotional outlet. 'Writing a journal,' said George Sand, 'means that facing your ocean you are afraid to swim across it, so you attempt to drink it drop by drop.' I didn't think I could drink one more drop. The Captain must have sensed the spiritual sloth of accidie oozing from the deck. 'Let's circumnavigate

Carna? Bit of history here, you know.' Carna is a small island almost plugging the entrance to Loch Teacuis. The loch empties into Loch Sunart to the west, the east channel so narrow that a stone could be thrown across at certain points. Here, in the aftermath of the 1745, Royal Navy sailing ships circumnavigated Carna towed by six or eight oared longboats in search of the fleeing Charles Edward Stewart. Every channel and inlet no matter how narrow was explored. The size of the Navy boats should have given me confidence but the pilot book had the final say as far as I was concerned. 'The passages either side of Carna are among the trickiest bits of rock-dodging any where on the West Coast.' The west channel is called Caol Ashadh Lic, which translated means 'the channel of the field of stones'.

'No, let's not,' I replied.

Loch Na Droma Buidhe

'Alright, we'll go into Drumbuie. There is only one rock at the entrance. And you will steer her in. Then we'll sit on deck and have a leisurely supper and watch the sun set.' I understood the Captain's intentions and respected him for it. With superhuman effort I complied. Drumbuie is one of the prettiest and safest anchorages in the West Coast. After the narrow entrance a little, almost perfectly round bay opens out. Birch and oak woods densely line the water's edge of cream white rock, heather clad on top, ochre lichen and rich brown seaweed dipping into the sea below. Facing down the seaward end of the Sound of Mull, the flat line of a far off outlying island is on the horizon. The loch of Drumbuie is daily washed by the Atlantic. Despite the hundreds of fish cages over its shoulder in Loch Sunart there is not a mite of scum on its clear waters. It could have been different. An application was made for a fish farm in the south-west corner of Drumbuie but the Coastguard fought the application on the grounds that the anchorage was a vital refuge for small craft, and won. That is why the lichen on the rocks was as brilliant in colour as that of the Outer Hebrides; fading searock lichen is an indicator of polluted waters.

Unfortunately, from the Captain's perspective, and now my moody own, Drumbuie is exceedingly popular with the yachting and cruising fraternity. 'Easy to get into and just that little bit excitingly far from Tobermory,' informed the Captain, cynically. By early evening, 'commuter time', the loch was ringed with all shape and size of vessel. We manoeuvre to anchor by *Genara*, a converted Grimsby trawler to starboard. She is big and rounded, her ample stern overhanging; the hull painted dark almost black-green with a fine red line at the gunwale. 'Now that is *the* boat. Will do anything, go anywhere,' said the Captain. I'd heard this before somewhere, sometime …

I am at the helm, the Captain at the bow, anchor poised. The hot day's water calm and transparently green but wickedly deceptive in temperature. On our port side is a mini gin palace, cockpit cocktail awning and all. A smaller version lay to its port. Its Skipper and crew are dinghying over for drinks on the big gin palace.

The Captain's ruse to keep me occupied is rehabilitating. Might have a gin and tonic myself soon enough. My glide in for anchor laying is with perfect timing, the Captain indicates such from the bow. 'Reverse a little,' he instructs for the final settling tug of the anchor. Inexplicably the engine cuts out. But no matter, we are safely anchored. We smile at each other. 'Well done!' says the Captain.

The engine has cut out because I have reversed over the slack painter of the dinghy which is now tightly wound round *Anassa*'s prop and shaft. There is no smiling now. The Captain spends an age hanging over the gunwale of *Anassa* poking and prodding the Celtic knotwork of the painter with the boat-hook then getting into the dinghy for better visibility and leverage. I have to hold the dinghy steady, which is no mean feat when 14 stone of man is alternately tugging and trying to loosen an immovable object an arm's length below water. Cold water. I keep suggesting tying the boatknife which the Captain lovingly sharpens on a daily basis to the boat-hook and 'just cut through the bloody rope!' This is not received kindly. 'Never, *never* cut a rope unless it is absolutely necessary!' The Captain is very angry. I hold back giggling hysteria. This so important rope. The cockpit lockers are full of them.

The absolute worst happens to the Captain next. The Skipper of *Genara* dinghies over to help. 'Those lobster creel ropes …' he sympathises. Nothing is said aboard *Anassa*. *Genara* and the Captain recognise each other from Outward Bound days. They talk over old times, the delicate issue of the rope temporarily suspended. Finally it is addressed. *Genara* offers to get his wet suit. The prop shaft needs to be manually turned back and forth to find which end of the rope leads to loosening. The Captain tries from within the engine casing first and it works. In time the painter comes clear. In two bits – much to the Captain's disappointment.

Genara's sympathy evaporated somewhat on discovering we had fouled on our own dinghy painter. I vociferously took all the blame, of course, Presbyterian child that I am, and relapsed into *mea culpadom* for the rest of the night, truly fed up of boats and ropes and their capriciousness. The gin palace had watched everything from on high.

'Actually, I stole that rope,' said the Captain, almost repentantly, whilst we ate a cold scratch supper and I accepted that gin and tonic had never existed on *Anassa*.

It was another night of restless fears. I woke in the dark, fighting claustrophobia, clawing and scratching my way out of the blackest bottomless pit, trying to call out a name that would not come. On deck the sky was paling to the east behind a solitary grey cottage on a rise at the head of the loch. Carna loomed dark and menacing. The water of the loch was evilly black-smooth. A strange elliptical structure all of 30 feet high was silhouetted further up the rise behind the cottage. No lights shone in the house or boats in the bay. What was this weird thing beginning to glint in the lightening sky? Two bands of curved stainless steel met at the top and bottom of an upright pole with two lateral spars quarter way up and down the pole keeping the ellipse in perfect form. Many wire stays held all in place. An artistic installation? The cottage, home of some eccentric sculptor who was not

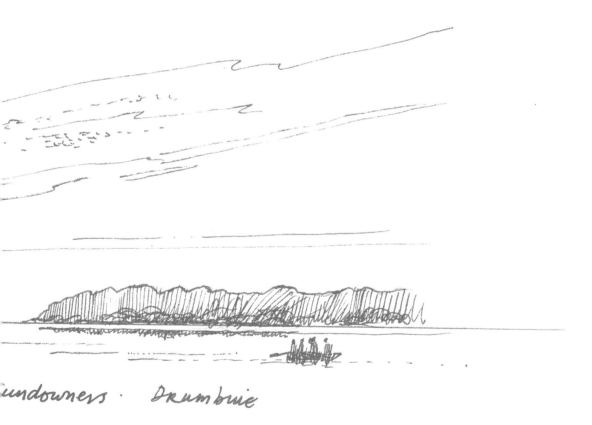

undowners · Drumbuie

·Drumbuie.·

desirous of clients? The dead end track to the cottage bumps and dips and winds west and south about six miles to the single track metalled road at Drimnin, thence to Lochaline, the nearest village, a further nine miles. Maybe the erection was totemic, the creation of a religious cult, warding off with an upended evil eye those who entered its territory. How easily was everyone else sleeping in their waterborne bunks in the Bay of Drumbuie?

In the full light of day the structure fairly shone and lost its threatening look. After a late breakfast I was driven to find out the truth of the matter. Using a yachtie ploy, we rowed to the shore with empty water containers, the excuse to approach the strange house and whover was within. Like guerrillas we cautiously circled the rise and came round the back of the property. The erection was bigger and more of a mystery. Even the Captain had no notion as to its purpose. Tentatively, we went round the corner of old steadings rebuilt with sympathetic render. The yard was filled with trays of seedlings and bedding plants but no one about. A four-wheel drive was parked at the gable end of the cottage. Not without a little apprehension we came round the side of it. In the second I had a glimpse through a window of the woman eating at a table within, her head turned and with a cry of delight she was at the door, saying, 'Come in, come in! Have a glass of wine! I'm at my lunch, you'll not mind if I finish. Fresh pork chop all the way from Fort William this morning but I only got one – can't let it go to waste! Sit down, sit down!' We were received completely, unconditionally, like long lost friends. J, white ruffled hair, benignly rounded, was dressed *à la provençale*, a long navy-blue spotted dress revealing a kindly bosom under a well-worn cailleach cream apron. Gardener's hands filled our glasses with fine red wine. A West Highlander by birth and up-bringing, she told the story of how she and her husband had taken thirty-two years of commuting from Glasgow to build up the ruins and gardens and how she spent all her time here now that her husband was semi-retired. All the while my eyes greedily feasted on the old familiar pine panelling walls, the black stove, the driftwood shelf brackets and coathooks, rows and rows of jars of just made raspberry jam still hot to the touch, the clutter of a house of great character and love. And I am reminded of my old home and way of life on the island, left for ever, and am so frightened. Where am I going? The weeks on *Anassa* have lost me my identity, my sense of place, both so importantly, sacrosanctly, integrally intertwined all my life. This kindly woman is the ghost of my times irrevocably past. Where now? What have I done?

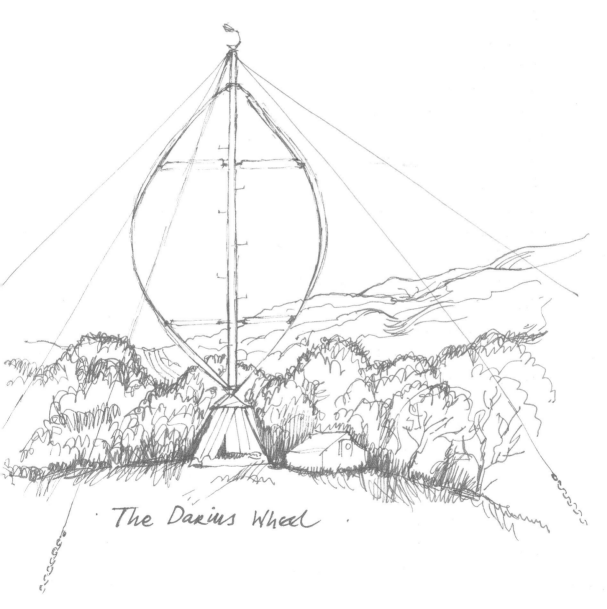

The Darius Wheel

'Now,' said J, quite unaware of the amanuensis of her being, 'it is my day for house cleaning. My daughter and her boyfriend are coming tomorrow. Away you go to the garden and pick whatever fruit is in excess to take to the boat. I'm fed up making raspberry jam and we're still eating last year's redcurrant jelly.' As she points out the direction of the fruit and vegetable garden I deliver my prepared speech. 'I know you must be fed up with yachties that come on the pretext of asking for water when all they want to know is *what* is that thing behind the house.' 'Oh! that? That is the Darius Wheel, the wind generator. C [her husband] made it. It is model No. 7. Still being perfected, I think. If I don't like the look of people who turn up at the door,' she added, as an afterthought, 'I say I am a member of a religious cult. That soon sends them packing.'

We pick redcurrants, blackcurrants and raspberries till our hands are stained and our bellies full. Rhubarb and rooted herb replacements for *Anassa* fill other bags. We do some weeding but there is little not under control.

When we return J is sitting outside in the sun. 'Wonderful, no midges!' And then she says, 'I've run a bath for you. I'll just get a last bucket of hot water before you get in.' I am so affected by this woman's delight in sharing her piece of heaven with us, I lie long in the deep old-fashioned bath and let the tears stream down my face. I was once like her. Who am I now?

Both the Captain and I were deeply affected by our experience at J's that afternoon. It was as though the Darius Wheel drew us to find the factual answer to its purpose, but in so doing drew us in to look for other answers. Answers to a journey which was threatening to disintegrate. Answers to ourselves. Neither of us had realised how tired and stretched we had become. And in directions as diverse as the different agendas that lay ahead of us when *Anassa* was finally tied up and we went our separate ways. It took someone else's kindness and generosity of spirit to touch us and see the lack in our own. We had both been trying to achieve too much. Not just in the physical journey but in our sometimes hard-pressed personal relationship. *Anassa*, beautiful as she was, was far too small for the two of us. And I had learned that whatever size the next boat was, it was not for me. All of this was unspoken between us but we both sensed the salvation of the journey had occurred.

The journey would take its own route from now on. We wended our way back down to the shore, stopping every so often to rest the water containers and scoop forefingers into a jar of J's new-made raspberry jam. It was still warm. And sweetly comforting. Sleep came easy that night. A sea change had occurred.

Anassa was alone in the bay next morning so late was our awakening. We had, for the first time ever, missed the tide. The overnight fishing line had a mackerel on each trace, however. A lazy brunch on deck of kedgeree, a read of my book (no longer *Iron Men, Wooden Women*, but the latest Aga Saga), a snooze in the sun, the Captain tinkering away at some nautical ploy … I could almost smell the sangria and olive groves.

As we rounded Auliston Point to enter the Sound of Mull I slowly turned my back on the thin blue line of the far off island.

The Sound is alive with cabbage butterflies. The early risers of Drumbuie anchorage are at play in sight of their beloved Tobermory. They dart back and forth. They will do this all day. The *Lord of the Isles*, hell-bent for Oban, overtakes our insignificance and rudely bashes us with her bow wash. Two of my fingers itch to retaliate but I wave a hand instead. No one waves back.

'We're not going up Loch Etive,' announced the Captain. 'We're getting off this motorway as soon as possible.' I didn't argue. Momentarily a tiny residual seed of contrariness composted in false pride and masochism struggled to sprout, but was quickly weeded out. There was no need to prove anything any more. Deirdre could keep her sorrows to herself.

It was a brilliant sail down the Sound. At last the good weather had come to stay. It was now August and the tilt of the summer begun. We so deserved this respite. Our wet and windbeaten skin soaked in sun oil and regeneration.

Lochaline was tempting to nip into but the Captain was running with the tide to Rubha an Ridre opposite Craignure and wanted to catch the slack to get us up the west stretch of the Lynn of Lorne. He had a remote spot in mind for the night.

Loch a'Choire

It was at Kingairloch in Loch a'Choire. A dolphin led us towards the silk-smooth water of the inlet. Diamante droplets catching the sun cascading from its languorous arching back. He had chummed *Anassa* all the way up the Lynn of Lorne.

'He's a bow rider, that one,' admired the Captain. 'Reminds me of the story of a dolphin called Pelorus Jack who between 1888 and 1912 used to meet and pilot ships across Admiralty Bay, North of French Pass between Wellington and Nelson, New Zealand. He became such an institution that in 1904 he was protected by legislation under a Sea Fisheries Act. Herman Melville cherished dolphins. In *Moby Dick* he wrote: "They are the lads that always live before the wind. They are accounted by a lucky omen. If you can withstand three cheers at beholding these vivacious fish, then heaven help ye; the spirit of godly gamesomeness is not in ye." Isn't that a wonderful quote? I feel exactly like that on sighting a dolphin!' And he gave out more than three rousing cheers. The dolphin definitely cocked an eye. 'He's most likely a solitary old male bottlenose. Like Fungi in Dingle Bay off the West Coast of Kerry in Ireland. Sometimes they adopt a section of coastline with its bays and inlets as their home range. Did you know that bottlenoses can swim at seventeen miles an hour because their bodies never get wet?' I did not. 'It is like this,' he went on to explain. 'They are constantly sloughing off and replacing their skins. That's how they never touch the water. They swim through a tight tunnel of shed skin. So they have no contact friction with the water which would slow them down. Brilliant, isn't it? And do you know they also carry around with them the equivalent of a loaded gun? They can immobilise or even kill their prey using bursts of high frequency sound. This means they can feed on prey that can out-distance or out-manoeuvre them. That is how the dolphin can have the occasional meal of salmon. Do you think Kingairloch Jack has had a feed of an escaped farmed salmon today?'

I did not. I did not believe a word of it. Loaded gun indeed! Kingairloch Jack had heard enough too and chose not to come into Loch a'Choire.

The loch is small like Drumbuie but surrounded by magnificent wild mountains which dictate a completely different atmosphere. I hope Daniell found this spot. He would have loved to exaggerate its majesty with more than a hint of stylised savagery. Quite hidden in trees at the head of the loch is Kingairloch House. A cottage or two on either shore make up the total of habitations. There is an air of desuetude in the silence of the landscape. A very large expensive French yacht from La Rochelle is the only other boat anchored for the night. It is dwarfed by the immensity of its surroundings. When the sun starts to slip behind the horseshoe of mountains, glens and corries darken with mysterious shadows as they have done since the end of the last Ice Age, 10,000 years ago. Maybe, right where *Anassa* is anchored, a Mesolithic hunter gatherer looked up from gutting fish in his skin boat to watch the exact same transformation of day to night as I was doing. He certainly did watch a sunset or two behind these hills, if more distantly, from Oban. At the end of last century, as building work expanded in the town, caves containing Mesolithic remains and artefacts of bone and antler tools were discovered in the cliffs of the former shoreline. Over these self-same mountains, westwards to Risga Island in Loch Sunart and at Barr River which flows into Loch Teacuis, similar remains were found. As the shadows in the glens and corries darken further I fancy I hear a wolf howl, a bear growl, the tap-tap of an antler hammer, a newborn baby cry.

We were going to eat and sleep up on deck so hot had been the day and early evening. The Captain had made an awning stretched over the boom and attached to port and starboard rails out of one of a pair of faded canvas curtains from the days of sun-blistered front doors. 'Brought for just such an occasion!' he beamed.

The Captain's curtain was raspberry, oatmeal and white striped, perfectly toning with the burgundy of the furled mainsail, the teak of the deck. A veritable Bedouin tent. We sat crosslegged under it and had couscous for supper, night light candles flickering like will o' the wisps at our feet until a buffeting rising wind threatened their survival. *Anassa* swung round to face the intruder coming from the east directly through the narrow entrance to the loch. In keeping with the stage set the wind was warm, blown from a distant desert.

As the stars travelled over the dome of the night sky, the warm wind rose to gusting, Force 5 to 6. A summer storm. The tent flapped ferociously and I have a memory of every so often the Captain sitting bolt upright for minutes at a time, like a cadaver in a burning coffin, muttering 'Anchor Watch!' I decide not to get involved until the tent is shredded. If the anchor did not hold we'd just be washed up on the shore which was conveniently very near. Being on deck and not trapped in the cabin gave me great confidence. It would be easy to jump. *Boreal 1* dealt with the situation according to her class. Every so often computer-activated bow thrusters edged her fractionally forward and took the strain off the anchor chain and stabilised the twisting furies of rogue waves with a ghostly purr of her engines uncontrolled by human hand or judgement. Lying on *Anassa's* deck was like hurtling sideways the length of Britain on a night sleeper train, the window wide open. The Night Steward brought tea and biscuits at dawn. We had survived. And so had the tent.

The wind was still strong but anchors never drag in the daylight, do they? It was a day for walking on terra firma and washing clothes and ourselves in a deep river. We found it winding down past Kingairloch House, heavy-leaved trees overhanging a pool. To swim in the sea can never compare to the silken caress of the waters of a Highland river. A freshwater loch will do but it can have murky peaty depths.

Refreshed, cleansed, we left the dripping clothes on low-down branches on the bank of the river and followed its course inland to the heart of the silent mountains. I knew that the particular route we took had not been trodden by contemporary man or his forebears. That is the fact and delight of the latitudinarianism of wandering in remote places. No foot has stood on that sod, that rock, that bog but mine, etc. John Ruskin says it all the time. I haven't worked out whether it is a good thing or not to identify with him. He certainly wrote tomes on landscape, mountainscape, cloudscape, seascape and man's relationship with it. It took him ten years which is not to validate all of his pontifications but demonstrates a genuine commitment to try to interpret and understand the influence on man of the physical environment that surrounds him. But was it only the Victorians who possessed the sunset? I think of my Mesolithic man. And woman. And their baby's first step in this glen.

The Captain and I create a primitive game. The rule is to walk as far into the amphitheatre of the hills as the sun shines on us. When we are in shadow we must immediately turn and go back down the strath with the last fingers of the sun on our back, hurrying, hurrying lest the shadow of the mountains catch us.

Ahead an old substantial ruin, miles from the Big House, stands testament to the agricultural fertility of the glen last century where now the deer freely roam. It had been the mill sited close by the burn that feeds the river downstream where our clothes drip dry. Brambles and nettles choke doorways that sacks of flour would have been lugged through to be heaved on to waiting carts. The miller's children running in and out the harvest hubbub of hard graft and adult ceilidh, racing to the hills, hands over their ears when duty called. The deer retreated to the high skyline looking down on all the burst of activity. Their descendants, who now watch us but not from so far a vantage point, are a living link with the folk of Kingairloch who annually came to the mill to sell, to buy, to work, to socialise. The people are long gone, unlike the deer, from their place of birth.

The burn rushes and convolutes over a smooth worn boulder into a jacuzzi pool. We strip off and like otters slip and slide into the pool, climbing out and up the boulder again for another watershute slide. And again and again and again. I think of the miller's children doing the same thing. Did they run home when the sun fell behind the stern mountains? We did. The midges, descendants too, had not had human blood for a long time.

Loch Leven

The voyage of *Anassa* was coming to an end. We could only afford a couple more days before 'real life' commitments dictated picking up the skins we had shed all those weeks previously. My feelings were still ambivalent about the new direction in which I would be heading, but what was the use in worrying? Our greatest fears are but noxious thoughts in our heads. Did a sea monster drag me down to the depths? No, I just let myself drown in the idea of it. I experienced legitimate fear on several occasions during the voyage. I learned to react to fearful situations *when* they happened and not when they *might*. I will remember that valuable lesson should I ever set foot on a boat ever again.

We thought to linger another day in Kingairloch. Actually climb one of those mountains before heading up Loch Linnhe to the Caledonian Canal where *Anassa* would be berthed for the winter. But I distinctly heard the call of voices from the Isle of the Dead in Loch Leven.

Up anchoring from Loch a'Choire was no easy matter, so embedded in thick mud was the anchor by the storm. No change of weather had come with its fury. If anything it was hotter and hazier. The Appin hills floated above pockets of sea mist soon to be burned through. It was 6am and we were the only souls alive, floating with the silent tide betwixt and between the lonely wild side of Loch Linnhe and the still-sleeping hotels and B&Bs of Appin, Ballachulish and Glencoe on the other side. As we get nearer, the first of the day's nose-to-tail traffic glitters on the road parallel to our passage. Civilisation.

The distinctive cone shape of the Pap of Glencoe is blue hazed behind the Meccano tracery of the Ballachulish bridge. Going under the bridge the tide at 7 knots sweeps us into Loch Leven with a flourish. To starboard Sgòrr Dhonuill, Sgòrr Dhearg, Sgòrr a'Choise and Meall Mór drape from the sky like pale blue velvet ruched curtains. Eilean Munde, the Isle of the Dead, passes to port. It thrusts up out of the loch, vertical cliff-edged except for the east end which fragments into tiny islets and skerries facing the Pap of Glencoe and the white line of a caravan site a mile up the loch. Its total size is no more than the average graveyard. Ancient trees and tombstones crown its length.

We must go into Ballachulish first for supplies. The noise and speed of traffic is bewildering and shocking. Neither of us, we realise, has been behind the wheel of a car for six weeks. Sweaty tourists, wearing white and acid green and yellow and red outfits hurt the eye. A modern Visitor Centre dominates the landscaped site of the old Ballachulish slate mines. 'Mystery World' promises to tell of Scotland's Heritage in Folk Tales and tempts the tourists in one door, little dressed-up Vikings spill out of another fighting mock battles on the grass sloping down to the loch side. Doting parents photograph their horned-helmeted offspring. The Spar shop hadn't quite run out of everything.

How strange it was to anchor *Anassa* close by the island and know that mayhem was but a hundred yards away. The surrounding hills understandingly absorbed the fracas of civilisation and left us with deathly peace.

Many ancient burial grounds were established on small islands where wolves would be hard put to swim over and dig up corpses. Early stones were unhewn and uninscribed and nowadays many such island sites are unrecognisable. But Eilean Munde was lived on by one of St Columba's priests who sailed with his superior's blessing from Iona to Loch Leven in the sixth century. Mundus built a chapel that was still in use eight centuries later. For generations the MacDonalds of Glencoe, the Stewarts of Ballachulish and the Camerons of Lochaber ferried their dead over for burial and shared the maintenance of the graveyard, despite whatever bloody wars or disputes they entered into with each other on the mainland.

The Captain was not so sure about sleeping on the island. 'The midges will be hell,' he frowned. It also entailed several trips back and forth in the dinghy with tent, sleeping bags, extra duvet, primus stove. 'And mosquito coils, don't forget,' he added when he saw I was not to be deflected from my necromantic adventure. We dumped everything by the tiny shingled inlet just the width of the dinghy which is the only, and precarious, landing spot at the Glencoe end of the island. A yacht was anchored far off beyond the little necklace of islets and skerries. Selfishly, I prayed no one would land from it on to the island. Before pitching the tent we decided to explore the island. Trampled paths through knee-high rank grass led to some groups of stones, indicating irregular visitations such as ours, but the overall terrain was in desperate need of the MacDonalds, Stewarts and Camerons who regularly

Glencoe to the Isle
of the Dead

fm
'98

(56° 41'N 5°
13 Fathom

scythed their ancestors' last resting place. But what a collection of memorials! From earliest unhewn, unnamed stones to Victorian sepulchral extravaganzas and later more staid erections. Some groupings are shelved down the cliff edges, others sink into the concave meadow in the centre of the island. The most recent date I found was 1960. Fresh carnations in a jam-jar, a hole in the lid for each flower stalk, stood on a table stone. The chapel is on a rise facing Iona, just the walls left standing. Scrabbling under choking ivy and brambles there I found two mediaeval stones, Celtic patterned. There is also a very humorous, I'm sure not intended, tombstone erected to a Duncan MacKenzie. A kilted and targed figure is delivering the deathly sword thrust at a man falling from his horse. The inscription reads: 'The fate of an English Dragoon who attacked D.M.K. at the battle of Prest.p. where he fought

· Ballachulish ·

under Prince Charles Stuart.' At the time of the Massacre of Glencoe many MacDonald corpses were hidden under cairns of stone in the glen until it was safe to ferry them over to the island. What dreams would I have this night?

We were having difficulty in finding a spot to pitch the tent. I drew the line at actually sleeping in the body of the kirk, so to speak. We concentrated on the last rise before the little islands facing Glencoe. There were no upright stones but others there were, flat below the grass and totally unsympathetic to tent pegs. Disappointed, I had to give in and agree to getting all the gear back on board. The Captain's temper was fraying. It was long past suppertime. The first midge had appeared. Just as I turned to go down the rise my eye caught sight of a movement on the skerries. I looked again and made out two figures. Were they waving? Disgruntled with the failure of my ploy I desultorily waved back, hoping they would return to the far off yacht from which they had obviously swum. One of them carried a lilo.

Loading the dinghy, out of sight of the figures, we heard whimpering. 'That's crying!' said the Captain. Running back up the incline we could see the two figures hand in hand stumbling towards us over the terrain of seaweeded rocks, half splashing, half swimming the channels in between. One of them, the smaller, was crying but with only enough energy to emit mewling whimpers. The taller, lilo under-arm, pulled the slipping and sliding companion with the other, finally clinging onto a handhold on the cliff edge of Eilean Munde where we grabbed their ice-cold hands and hauled them up.

They were two young girls in skinny swimming costumes uncontrollably racked with shivering, their lips blue, words incomprehensible. Their bare feet were torn and bleeding. As the Captain said later they were in a serious state of hypothermia. He recognised their condition immediately. The blessed duvet and sleeping bags were wrapped round them immediately. The Captain told me to rub and rub their bodies through the fateful bedding and talk to them and reassure them all the while he was launching the dinghy. 'I'll get the Seagull from *Anassa* and batten it on the dinghy and take them back. Keep rubbing. Keep talking to them.'

As he was doing this and fuelling the outboard I found out what had happened. Annalis, 13, and Maryanna, 12, were Belgian and on holiday with their parents at the Glencoe caravan site. They had set off with the lilo, paddling it ahead of them to get to Eilean Munde. Their mother had read about the graveyard and told them all about it. They wanted to see it. But three-quarters of the way over they knew they were in trouble. They made for the shorter distance. Annalis's English was good. Slowly the enormity of the situation they could have been in dawned on her. 'You mean, *five* minutes and you would have left the island?' She repeated this at intervals, several times. The distance from Eilean Munde to Ballachulish was not far but a strong tide was running down the loch. In their exhausted condition they would not have survived. Her sister was incapable of any communication not because she had no English but she was still in shock. Did I imagine the blue was fading from their lips? I told Annalis to tell her sister they would be returning in the dinghy soon. 'Your parents will be worried,' I added.

'Oh no!' Annalis replied. 'We told my father where we were going …' This I relayed to the Captain who was hastily filling the petrol tank, with the intention of relaxing him before setting off with the sometimes unpredictable outboard motor. It had quite the opposite effect. '*What*?' he roared. 'He *let* them go? He should be horse-whipped! I'll do it myself when I get hold of him!' I trusted Annalis's English was not that good.

I watched the trio, the girls wrapped together in the duvet and a rug in the stern of the dinghy, get smaller and smaller as they made the long journey to Glencoe. With the binoculars I saw them land on the beach below the caravan site. No one came walking or even running to meet them. I expected the Captain to be bounding ahead of them raring to upbraid the father. I so looked forward to hearing all about it when the Captain got back. But he didn't move. He stood watching the girls, Annalis still clutching the lilo and her sister's hand, as they walked up the beach and then disappear into the trees of the caravan site.

I had the island and the dead to myself. How nearly there could have been two more corpses. What serendipitous God had brought us all together with such crucial timing? What hell had the Captain given the parents?

Slowly the little red *MacIntosh Coat to Anassa* came back to the island. The Captain was strangely quiet. I expected, and wanted, an overblown rendering of the confrontation I felt I had been denied. 'Why didn't you take the girls right up to the caravan door and hand them over to the parents, make sure they were safe?' I found his lack of contact with the parents incomprehensible. 'They were fine,' he replied. 'They knew what to do – stand in the shower, get warm.'

'But,' I expostulated, 'what if the showers weren't working, their parents not there?' I found my voice rising with incredulity. 'Will we ever know if they really got back home safe?'

'Of course they did. I watched them to the caravan door.' And he would say no more. It was as though he did not need the righteous indignation of pointing the finger of blame at anyone. I knew him well enough by now to know that the subject was firmly closed. But I was left with the enigma of wondering what had happened on that journey with the girls to defuse his raging anger. Would I ever know?

We slept in the Bedouin tent again, but very alive midges from the Isle of the Dead zeroed in, causing us to decamp to our bunks below. I dreamt that Annalis and Maryanna got right to the door of their caravan safely, their parents inside. Their father was very tall and dark-bearded.

Our last day aboard *Anassa* starts with the anchor up at dawn. And what a dawn. Lemon gold washes up from behind the Pap and the distant hills of Kinlochleven beyond. The platinum sky overhead is lightly flecked with tiny patches of cirrus. No light strikes the water yet save reflected lemon gold. *Anassa's* wake puckers it with little shadows of bronze black. Everything waits, breath held, for the brazen edge of the sun to sneak up over the darkness of the mountains and sear the lemon gold. When it comes I cannot look into its fierce expansion and look instead to where its first ray strikes the land. Dramatically it lights up Ballachulish church to port. To starboard its line is directly through the silhouetted pines of Eilean Munde. This can be no coincidence. Mundus chose his island as the elders of Ballachulish chose the site for their church because of this powerful phenomenon. I believe it to be so.

We are both very silent. The sun warms the back of my neck already. It will be another hot day. No wind. *Anassa* will doggedly motor out of Loch Leven, round to starboard through the Corran Narrows, up Loch Linnhe to Corpach and into the sea lock of the Canal. She'll climb Neptune's Staircase, a bit scruffy and war weary, but the onlookers will still be admiring. And finally she'll neatly steer into her waiting berth at Banavie. Her engine will cut with a sigh.

For *Anassa* there will be no depending on the tide for a long time. The Canal is to be closed for eight months for major maintenance. But like Annalis and Maryanna she will be safe.

I did find my new home on the mainland. Surrounded by trees and hills, not a loch or ocean in sight. Sometimes a rainstorm from the distant west sweeps over the hill behind the house and I believe I can smell the sea. I think back on the voyage which seems another life ago. I haven't heard from the Captain for months. He will be off on some ploy or other, exploring new mysteries, rejigging old ones.

And then I had a letter.

Karibu Guesthouse
Dar es Salaam
Tanzania
October 21st

Aye, Aye Crew,

Do you remember asking me why I didn't take the two Belgian girls right up to the caravan door and give the parents a severe lecture on risking the lives of their daughters?

Well, I understood your amazement because that's exactly what I would have done in the past. I would have verbally horse-whipped the parents for their negligence and felt fully justified.

I now see a different picture.

It's like this. Those girls had a life threatening experience; they were involved in the misery and discomfort of it for long enough for it to have had a lasting effect. They believed they were going to die. They might well have done had we not been where we were and they visible at that precise moment when you saw them. The girls realised this of their own volition. They told me so in the dinghy. They were incredibly lucky. They knew it.

I believe these girls experienced something uniquely personal; what they learned is their property, not transferable. It was the right, therefore, of those two young people to inform their parents in their own way as to what took place. Or perhaps say nothing at all.

My involvement, beyond ensuring the girls were safe and no longer at any risk, might have upset or angered the parents and jeopardised the girls' position. They could well have suffered as a result of further intervention by me.

While returning them in the dinghy, after you had begun their restoration, I emphasised the need for them to build and maintain body heat, suggesting a long hot shower and that they would be wise to go to bed early or straight away if they felt like it. They understood this as a consequence of their hypothermic state.

It may sound strange when viewing the proceedings from the outside, but I have a belief which emerged clearly at that time. It said that the whole of our boat journey with all of its delays from day one because of floods, through the running dry of diesel, the grounding and its subsequent holdups, the change of mind under Connel Bridge, The Rock, the 'careening', unscheduled time spent in Loch Nevis, the stillness of Drumbuie as well as the extra time enjoyed at Kingairloch, even the lack of wind, all this held us back from arriving on the island at the wrong time. We were there with sleeping bags, a travelling rug and a down duvet and standing on the only spot on the island where we could have seen those girls at the exact moment they came into sight and saw us too.

Fate? Perhaps coincidence?

No, I think it's a way of seeing. When you are confronted with something as stunning as this – how close those girls were to being dead – then your mind threads an explanation. The girls were finally safe, it never became a public drama, so they could deal with it in their individual ways.

Imagine the scenario when the press had got wind of it? Sure, our anonymity would have been interrupted, but imagine the possible abuse of privacy the girls might have suffered. Well, I think my intervention with the parents might well have generated something similar for the girls. So now, can you understand why I am content to be amazed at the experience we have shared?

Tanzania is an astounding country. The people have such an easy generosity of spirit.

Leaving Eilean Munde
The Isle of the Dead

(56° 41'N 5° 9'W)
15 Fathoms

I haven't got another boat yet or caught a coelacanth. Trains are fun in Tanzania, tho'.

You should come and experience it. We could journey to Congo to the place your father was born.

Yours over the yardarm,
The Captain

Postscript

The author would like to thank the following:

L. E. Bagshawe, N. I. Thomson, A. Ronaldson, Andrew Hothersall and Jeremy Sidgewick for their much valued comments, corrections and further information on *Anassa*.

Happy sailing, gentlemen

As soon as I saw a notice of your book, *Sea Change*, I found that I had to wonder whether there could be more than one small boat carrying a name in Homeric Greek. Now that I have a copy, I see that there aren't.

It must have been in 1956 that I was in Rangoon, working for ICI (Export) in their Rangoon office. I had a little money accumulated and thought that a boat a bit more ambitious than those at the Rangoon Sailing Club at the Inya Lake might be interesting. I got from Brian Kennedy, whom I had known in Bombay, a set of plans for his 'Slipway 5-tonner' and had them built by a Chinese builder, C. Ah Lam. He was interested in doing it since his and his workmen's experience was all in flat- or step-bottomed outboard runabouts and he wanted to see how a deep keel went together. And she was duly finished under the trees in his riverside yard . . . We found more or less everything locally – lead for the keel from Mawchi, held on with bolts made from a scrap phosphorbronze propeller shaft and teak for all the timberwork. Steaming and bending the timbers gave Ah Lam much trouble and quite a few broke. Unfortunately, I never managed to find a suitable inboard engine and we had to make do with an outboard working in a trunk, which was never very satisfactory, as it was apt to smother itself in its own exhaust. I gave her the name 'Anassa' partly as a sort of pun with the Pali *anatta*, the Buddhist principle of 'no-self', which I thought might be *mingala* and auspicious.

In the early '60s in the Ne Win era it looked as though my employment would be coming to an end soon and the question arose what to do with the boat and a solution appeared in the shape of Doug Young and Tommy Thomas, who thought that they would like to try to sail her back to England. They set off, but I'm afraid that they found that they were less compatible than they had thought and the project was abandoned in Colombo and the 'Anassa' was shipped to England and disposed of.

L. E. Bagshawe

***

My father, Innes Thomson, owned 'Anassa' from 1960 to 1971. He 'found' her lying in Whites yard at Cowes in the Isle of Wight in a fairly neglected condition, painted an overall 'drab' aircraft grey, and after negotiations, purchased her from the owners who had her built in the Far East and sailed her back to England.

She was shipped by lorry to Leith and after restoration work was launched there and sailed in the Firth of Forth, based at Granton for a year or two, with the occasional summer trip through the Forth and Clyde canal to the West Coast. Initially, her power unit comprised an outboard motor mounted in an internal 'well' in the cockpit, but this had many drawbacks, including the space taken up by the installation, the smoke fumes generated when motoring, and the general unreliability of outboards in the 1960s.

In 1961 an air-cooled Lister diesel inboard was installed and was such a success that in 1965 it was replaced with a larger and more powerful version of the same engine.

In 1962, with the closure of the Firth and Clyde canal imminent, Father decided to base her permanently on the Clyde, where she remained for the rest of his ownership. Her regular summer mooring was at McGruer's at Clynder and she spent her winters at McAlister's yard at Dumbarton.

Father thereafter cruised fairly extensively on the Clyde and West Coast, rounding both the Mull of Kintyre and passing through the Crinan Canal for his summer cruises, which took him round Mull, to the Small Isles, and as far north as Badachro in Wester Ross.

N. I. Thomson

***

I am writing to ask you to take pity on King Canute. In this country he is made out to be stupid enough to start arguing with the tide. The story really is that he was tired of his courtiers treating him as semi-divine so he sat on the beach to show them that he was only human and the tide would not obey him.

A. Ronaldson

***

… The recounting of the circumstances surrounding the naming of 'Macintosh Coat to Anassa' reminded me of this attached article from the journal of the Cruising Association.

> The prototype rubber boat that Peter Halkett began to
> develop . . . in 1842 was oval in shape, some 7ft 4in long
> and 3ft 5in broad, with an inboard space 3ft 5in by
> 1ft 4in. He called it the 'cloak-boat' because it was
> ingeniously glued within the lining of a 9ft-wide

semicircular mackintosh cloak! When afloat, the edges
of the cloak folded inwards to enable access to pockets
containing a rubber air pump (the craft could reputedly
be inflated in 30 seconds), a puncture repair kit,
inflatable paddles and even a walking stick which
contained an umbrella sail! The first experimental trip
made by Halkett in the cloak-boat was along the 11-mile
stretch of the Thames from Kew to Westminster, during
the course of which he was nearly run down by several
metropolitan paddle-steamers. By 1848 the published
prospectus of the boat stated that he had subsequently
paddled it at Brighton, Plymouth, Spitzbergen and
Brighton again.

Boats, Boffins and Bowlines, by George Drower

Andrew Hothersall

***

You quote a verse from 'The Log of the Blue Dragon' . . . the poet was not
C. C. Lynam himself but my uncle, Arthur Hugh (A. H. S.), who together with
my father (F. S.) wrote many of the verses. They were among many young men,
ex-pupils, friends and family, who crewed the little *Blue Dragon* and her larger
successors.

Jeremy Sidgewick
Captain RN (Rtd)

Nimium Ne Crede Experto
(A Libel)

'This narrow strait' (the Sailing Directions said),
Is full of rocks and difficult to enter;
Whirlpools are common here at every tide;
There are unchartered reefs on every side
And currents (twenty knots) along the centre.'
'Come,' said the Skipper, 'we will go in there.'
(We went in there.)

'There is no sand,' (the Sailing Directions said),
'The anchorage is thoroughly unsafe.
There is no shelter from the frequent squalls,
Save on the west, among the overfalls.
Boats should go on to Loch MacInchmaquaif.'
'Come,' said the Skipper, 'we'll anchor here.'
(We anchored here.)

From *The Log of the Blue Dragon* by C. C. Lynam (1903);
verse by Arthur Hugh Sidgwick